Westchester

Westchester

Portrait of a County

Alex Shoumatoff

Vintage Books
A Division of Random House, Inc.
New York

First Vintage Books Edition, December 1990

Library of Congress Cataloging-in-Publication Data
Shoumatoff, Alex.
Westchester : portrait of a county / Alex Shoumatoff.
p.   cm.
Reprint. Originally published: New York : Coward, McCann & Geoghegan, 1979.
ISBN 0-679-73327-2 (pbk.)
1. Westchester County (N.Y.)—Description and travel.   I. Title.
F127.W5S53   1990
917.47'2770443—dc20   90-50437
CIP

Portions of this work appeared
in slightly different form in *The New Yorker*.

Manufactured in the United States of America
10 9 8 7 6 5 4 3 2 1

To brother Nick,
whose love of Westchester
is a continuing inspiration.

Contents

Part One *The Land*

A Word of Explanation 15

1 *A Hawk's-Eye View of Westchester County* 17

2 *The Woods* 23

3 *Emeralds and Erratics* 33

4 *Some Punkins* 49

5 *The View from Brookside* 65

6 *Bitten by a Copperhead* 75

7 *A Year on the Land* 83

Part Two The People

8   The Hub of Northern Westchester   105

9   The Days of the Big Houses   121

10   Crumbling Strata   131

11   From Far Away Across the Foam   149

12   The Lower Tier   161

13   Prototypes   175

14   Two Roads   189

15   The Brutal Commute   201

16   Coming Attractions   207

"But it is illusion to think that there is anything fragile about the life of the earth; surely this is the toughest membrane imaginable in the universe, opaque to probability, impermeable to death. We are the delicate part, transient and delicate as *cilia*."

—Lewis Thomas, *The Lives of a Cell*

Part One
The Land

A Word of Explanation

"We exist but in a landscape."—Constable.

For the last few years I've been devoting myself to the study of Westchester County, New York. I've tried to get a sense of all the forces, cultural and natural, past and present, that make the place what it is today. It hasn't been an easy image to assemble, nor have I had much success explaining what I've been doing or why I undertook to do it in the first place.

I've done my best to get my facts straight, but I must confess that, in themselves, "the facts" don't really interest me. We can conceive of as many facts, after all, as we can combinations of words, and anyone who thinks he can string together a bunch of them and pass it off as "the truth" is in deep trouble, as far as I am concerned. How a writer selects and arranges his "facts" invariably reflects his own preconceptions and prejudices and those of his time.

So if I've made a few errors, they're all my doing. I've chosen my facts more for their resonance than for their "truth." Each chapter is a collection of facts that somehow sing to me, and the sixteen chapters that follow have approximately the same relationship to each other as cuts on a record. By the time you get to the end of the album you will, I hope, without too much strain on the

15

ears, have gotten a pretty good idea of what's happening around here. In no way should my pronouncements be associated with any of the three other people in Westchester who bear the name Shoumatoff. Above all I don't wish to embarrass or make life difficult for the people who graciously allowed me to interview them; in many cases, their names have been changed.

I'd also like to urge the reader at the outset to regard my vignettes of the various settlements in Westchester not as definitive statements, but rather as random samplings, even (particularly in the case of the Lower Tier communities) as fleeting impressions. I do not mean to imply that all people in the upper class of Bedford are snobs—there are some wonderful people in that stratum—or that all people in Scarsdale are aggressive, or that all people in Mount Vernon are on welfare. No one is more leery of sweeping sociological generalities than I.

Besides the people whose names appear in the text, I'd like to thank the following for their various contributions to this project: Christina Rainsford for explaining that the automobile was the catalyst for the return of the forest, the Marsh Sanctuary for providing me with a roof, Mike Steinfelt, Mrs. Knapp, and Mrs. Hughes at the Mount Kisco Library for getting obscure books in a hurry, Jeanette R. Stuke, Captain and Mrs. Gerard Wood, Walter Ragonese, Philip Sharlach, Kay Oliver. The Dick Boyd family, including Pop Buselle, Mr. and Mrs. Worthington Mayo-Smith, Tony Buzzanco, Warren Balgooyen, Kaye Anderson, my father who did his best to make sure my statements were responsible, my mother who fed me juicy social tidbits, the Honorable Albert Marchigianni, Mary Robbins, Lewis Mumford, Dick Andrews, Lucy Stanton, Arthur Bernhardt, Gerry Koshar, Tom de Zengetita, Mr. and Mrs. Donald Marshal, Wilhelmina Waller, Dorothy Hinitt, Susan Braudy, Julio de la Torre, Bill Bondi, Mike Tkacz, Tim Ferris, Harriet Lions, Ginny Weinland, Dr. Harold Clum, Carl Specht, Craig Hibbon (the last three of the Kitchawan Field Station of the Brooklyn Botanical Garden), Foxy Gwynne for accompanying me to the monastery, Angela Thorne for going along to the Life Savers factory.

I would like finally to thank the pretty girls at the Midnite Diner for feeding me at least once a day while I was holed up writing this book.

1 A Hawk's-Eye View of Westchester County

I thought I ought to take a look at it from the air, to confirm my suspicions about the place. So I got hold of my friend Haddon, who has a plane—a little Aeronca Champ that he owns in partnership with six others, up in Dutchess County. "It's a real putt-putt but it does the job for this sort of thing," he said as he went around untying the moorings and kicking the tires.

You couldn't have asked for a better day. There wasn't a shred of cloud in the whole Northeast, as far as I could see, just a little haze on the horizon. As we took off a parachutist was hanging over the airfield like a spider on a thread. Then we soared over the high walls and bleak wards of the Greenhaven State Prison. "That's where the electric chair is," Haddon yelled back, chewing a pink wad of Dentyne under a set of headphones.

The dying rural landscape of Putnam County opened below us. Some of the land had been in corn but it was October and the fields were brown and empty. Some had been let go, to be overrun with blueberries, brambles, and cedar. Here and there along a gleaming watercourse an abandoned car was decomposing. Desultory ribbon development lined the major thoroughfares. Up on the ridges and in the rest of the lowlands it was mostly trees.

To the south it was nothing but trees. Our shadow was racing over the most richly diversified deciduous forest in the world: forty-two hundred species of plants from ferns on up. The leaves had been down for several weeks now, persisting only on the scattered brown domes of oaks and the yellow fountainheads of weeping willows.

Over the steeples and weathered storefronts of Brewster, Haddon steered the Champ south. To the right was the Hudson; to the left, coming in a flatter angle, the Long Island Sound; two blue lines headed for a meeting at some point lost in the haze. Ahead of us was the subject: Westchester County. There was nothing spectacular about it, no hint of its rich human diversity or its intense natural beauty. It was just a jumble of bumps. Rocks of different hardness weathering at different rates had left knobs of granite and gneiss, midslopes of schist, and bottomlands of mud-covered marble.

The peninsula that narrowed before us is known as the Manhattan Prong. It is the tail end of a geologic sub-province of the Appalachians called the New England Upland. The Manhattan Prong breaks off at Manhattan Island. Another prong of the New England Upland ends in Reading, Pennsylvania. Between them lies a younger sub-province called the New Jersey Lowland. Most of the Manhattan Prong—449 square miles of it—is in Westchester County.

We held to a thousand feet. Ahead, two red-tailed hawks were playing tag in the thermals. They seemed used to planes and banked easily to a lower level as we approached. "They can outmaneuver us," Haddon yelled back. "We could never catch them." He pointed down to the Tilly Foster iron mine, abandoned for years, briefly resurrected when an attempt was made to raise mushrooms in the shaft. Four cement silos were fastened like barnacles to the side of the same hill.

Our plan was to follow the Harlem Valley, which runs from Brewster clear to the Bronx and is the prong's most prominent feature. Civilization has always favored this valley. The main Indian paths ran up it, along the riverbanks. By 1850 the tracks of the New York and Harlem Railroad Company had been laid in it. A string of depots, mainly for picking up milk, came into being, and hamlets grew up around them. Today their names are etched into the subconscious of every weary commuter who rides on the

18

Harlem Division: Tuckahoe, Scarsdale, Hartsdale, North White Plains, Valhalla, Pleasantville, Mount Kisco, Bedford Hills, Katonah. In the 1930s the Saw Mill River Parkway came up the Harlem Valley. It was the golden age of roadbuilding, and the Bronx and Hutchinson River parkways had already been extended up the two other major valleys of the Manhattan Prong. The river parkways are not only efficient but beautiful, not just roads but greenbelts conserving important watersheds.

From the air the Harlem Valley was not the clean, straight trench I had imagined it to be. Winding and weaving at various elevations, it drains most of central Westchester, but is not the creation of one river. Several rivers, none named Harlem, cut in and out of it.

Now we were over Somers. Haddon pointed to a knoll smothered with the elegant, earth-colored units of an adult condominium called Heritage Hills of Westchester. Each unit faced at a slightly different angle, and on each patio, gripping the armrests of their sun deck chairs and taking in the views, sat a motionless elderly couple.

Still in the north-county, we were beyond the gravitational pull of New York City. Ninety-five percent of the land, it seemed, was woods. The rest was open: a few farms and orchards, mostly "holdovers" which had been in the same family for generations. To the west, in a distant meadow somewhere in South Salem, three riders in velvet helmets were taking a succession of jumps. Horses are to the Salems what sailboats are to the Hamptons. To the east, in Yorktown Heights and Baldwin Place, the landscape was more democratic: There were vast shopping malls and new subdivisions with the grass still coming in between the rows of identical houses.

The valley beneath us bifurcated and became two valleys. The one to the right was filled with water—the long, shimmering crescent of the New Croton Reservoir, held back by a mighty dam which took seventeen years to build and upon completion in 1907 was the second-largest piece of hand-hewn masonry in the world. Thousands of Italians were imported for the job. Today one out of every three of Westchester's 870,000 inhabitants is likely to have Italian blood and many are descended from people whose first home in America was a shack beneath the Croton Dam.

We took the left-hand valley and followed it to Katonah, which

19

looked like, and still is, a quiet upstate town. South of Katonah, homing in now on north-central Westchester, we could no longer claim to be in the country. We were getting into that transitional area between the suburbs and the country for which the late A. C. Spectorsky invented the term exurbia. It was, as Senator Proxmire has characterized his native Lake Forest, Illinois, "a very, very fortunate environment." We could see signs of affluence everywhere: big houses, lush gardens, swimming pools, tennis and paddle tennis courts. It was not new money. The occupants of this landscape spoke, dressed, furnished their homes, planted their grounds, and in general patterned their lives after the rural English aristocracy. Their byword was quiet good taste.

"Look at this mansion coming up," Haddon said, pointing to an approaching hilltop. The stone and slate-tiled affair below, with its two-acre greenhouse, squash court, and indoor pool and tennis court, had been designed by the firm of Frederick Law Olmsted, the man who designed Central Park. It is one of the best of the big houses, built by one of the great turn-of-the-century fortunes. But like many of the others it lies empty. Nobody lives like that anymore, with flocks of servants and fleets of cars.

From the air we could see how the social strata of the exurbs conformed with the geological strata. This is a fairly common phenomenon in the United States. One finds it also, for example, in Los Angeles and its foothills. Down in the valley was blue-collar Mount Kisco, with its light industry, high-rise apartments, housing projects, and mini-ghetto. This was where the blacks and the most recent immigrants—Argentines, Greeks, and others in lower socioeconomic circumstances—lived. They did things like clean houses and work in factories. On the hillsides the petit bourgeois had collected in subdivisions. They were immigrants with more seniority—Italians and Irish who had been around for a generation or two and ran a grocery store or had cornered a service like plumbing. As you got higher the people got fewer and richer. They belonged to what sociologists sometimes call the "lower-upper" class. The richest and most aloof lived in big hilltop houses. They were known in the local nomenclature as hilltoppers.

Chappaqua. We were getting into the hard-core suburbs, the bedroom communities that form the image most people have of Westchester: Pleasantville, Thornwood, Greenburgh, Mamaroneck, New Rochelle. This was the realm of civic-minded wives and no-nonsense houses—one-third for living, one-third for sleeping, one-third for the car. But Chappaqua itself was an older, more gracious suburb. There was enough land—an acre or two per residence—to support a riotous biota and to live in privacy—but not so much that one felt guilty. A certain amount of eccentricity was tolerated. One didn't have to mow the lawn every week if one didn't feel like it. Trees were still the major component. We were still in the great forest north of the city. The development was still well-adjusted. There was still wild land in Chappaqua—woodland lakes near Twin Ridges that could as well have been in the Adirondacks.

Below the Cross-County Expressway, Route 287, the dividing line between the north- and south-county, rashes of little dots, each one representing a dwelling, began to get serious. "The land's running out," Haddon shouted back. But it was still surprisingly open—maybe forty-five percent—considering that one-tenth of the people in the United States live in a fifty-mile radius. Only at the very lower edge of the county—Yonkers, Mount Vernon, Pelham—was it perhaps ninety percent concrete and houses. Here and there we could see the cancer of urban decay, and nice old neighborhoods going to seed. A few last patches of green asserted themselves along Hillview Reservoir, and the Yonkers Raceway, then it was all swallowed up by the dismal sprawl of the Bronx.

Having by now overflown Westchester, Haddon turned the Champ around and headed north over the Hudson River. We glimpsed the big Fisher Body and Chevrolet plants along the river, long barges plowing tediously upstream through the muddy brown water, the Armour-Steiner octagonal house in Irvington, the sweeping curve of the Tappan Zee Bridge, an apple orchard, an osprey, a forest fire in progress across the river, the mostly abandoned Sing Sing, penitentiary at Ossining, sidestreams meandering through vast reed-infested marshes, swarms of seagulls at the Croton Point Dump. Under the bridge to Route 9 and Peekskill, we could see the shanties hillbillies have built out over Annsville Creek, an estuarine arm of the river.

The Hudson Gorge, where the river narrows at Bear Mountain, was superb. Few people realize it, but the Hudson is a true fjord—a river canyon deepened below sea level by glacial action. The

21

Hudson is tidal as far north as Troy. The only other fjord in the northeast is in Maine.

Before I knew it, the little airfield in Dutchess County had come into view, and after getting permission to land we started to come in low over the Greenhaven State Prison. The last thing we saw from the air was some of the inmates out in the yard, playing basketball in their denims.

2 *The Woods*

At nine hundred and thirty-eight feet Cross River Mountain is one of the highest points in Westchester, almost high enough to be what topographers call a "bald." Stunted oaks with a fragrant understory of mountain laurel grow on it, and on its south side pitch pines cling to exfoliated granite ledges on which pilot black snakes drape their coils during the month of May. On top of the mountain is an abandoned fire tower. Graffiti festoon its girders, and the windows of the booth that crowns the structure, seventy feet up, have all been knocked out. On a good day from the tower you can see the eastern tip of Long Island, the jumbled beginnings of the Catskill Mountains beyond the Hudson River, and the needles of the New York skyline catching the sun fifty miles to the south.

A stiff breeze numbed my companions and me as we stood in the booth combing the October sky with field glasses. We were half a dozen assorted bird-watchers looking for hawks. Tens of thousands of migrating hawks funnel down through the Hudson Valley at this time of year. But the sky that morning was leaden and hawkless. Only screaming bands of bluejays patrolled the oak canopy below, and a few brave monarch butterflies, on their way to Mexico, drifted past. The hawks were not moving, and we were getting cold.

"Too bad my brother isn't here any more, with his white gas stove," I said. In 1966 my brother had joined the New York State Department of Environmental Conservation. They'd given him a badge, a pair of binoculars, a map, and a radio, and told him to go up on Cross River Mountain and keep an eye out for smoke. For two seasons he lived at the foot of the tower in a small cabin heated by wood and illuminated by kerosene. I brought him food and helped him build an outdoor shower. This is how it worked: You climbed up a ladder on the side of the stall with a bucket of water which you poured into a washtub with a plugged-up hole in the middle of it. Then you stood underneath and pulled a chain that removed the plug and released the water into a second tub with dozens of holes punched into it, and gradually the water filtered down and gave you a shower. But since he had to haul his water from the base of the mountain, my brother didn't use the contraption very often.

One night in July I was walking up the mountain to pay him a visit when a coyote stepped into the road fifty feet in front of me. The animal stood for a full thirty seconds in the moonlight, with its ears pricked up like radar scanners, staring at me insolently; then disappeared into the laurel. Fresh from the West, I was positive in my identification. A few years earlier Stanley Grierson, Westchester's most active field naturalist until the ecology boom spawned a half dozen of them, had watched a coyote give birth in the woods behind his house. Maybe this was one of her cubs.

Up in the booth my brother spent his time figuring out how to strum the autoharp like Maybelle Carter and dealing with the public. Most people asked the same questions. My brother wrote down the answers to the twenty most common ones and when someone would ask, "Say, what's that body of water down there?" he would say "Number 6" and point to his list, and after Number 6 would be "Lake Kitchawan." Sometimes they would ask, "Say, don't you ever get lonely up here?" and he would mutter, "No. Number 20." Number 20 was "How could you get lonely with a view like this?" One woman was put off by the numerical treatment. "He must work for the state," she whispered to her husband loud enough for my brother to hear. "The federal observers are more courteous."

After my brother left, the Department of Environmental Conservation hired another observer who couldn't take the isolation and left after three months to join the Hare Krishnas; in 1970, it closed down the tower altogether. Heavy vandalism during the November-to-April off-season, budget cuts that emptied half the firetowers in the state, and increased reliance on air patrol prompted the decision. My brother now runs a nature museum at the bottom of Cross River Mountain, in the Ward Pound Ridge Reservation, and that morning I was leading one of his scheduled "hawk walks." My anecdotes about the firetower drew a few dispirited chuckles but did nothing to alter the fact that there were no hawks in the sky. One man had driven all the way from the Bronx to see them.

To avoid having the expedition turn into a complete bust, I suggested that we go into the woods and look for mushrooms.

"Would you believe," I said as we were coming down from the tower, "that a hundred years ago, there were fewer woods in Westchester than there are today?" We paused to look out. In every direction the view was filled with trees; only a few houses, clearings, and reservoirs broke the dominion of woods. It was not hard to believe. "Almost all this was clear," I said, waving all around me.

Primeval Westchester, as the settlers found it, was, like the entire Northeast, deep forest. The trees were "of great magnitude," as John James Audubon wrote. It was so dark beneath them that there was "little underwood," and there were few deer because there was no browse for them to eat except where lightning, windthrow, or Indian fire had made a clearing. On a typical acre there were eighty enormous trees. The settlers girdled them, then, when they were dead, went at them with axes. It took one man one year to clear one acre. Most of the wood went up in smoke.

By the 1880s, after two centuries of persistent attack, Westchester County was eighty percent clear, according to a land study conducted then. To judge from early photographs, it was a bleak wasteland of boulder-strewn pastures and long stone fences. Only on the ridge and hilltops and down in the ravines, where it was too steep and rocky to farm, were the woods intact; and in the fall the farmers would go into them with ox-drawn carts and cut the trees they needed to see them through winter. The land was so open, the late Gustavus T. Kirby, a famous amateur sportsman in Bedford, recalled in his memoirs, that as a child he would sit on top of Guard Hill, pull out the sections of a spyglass, and focus on the construction of the Brooklyn Bridge, forty miles to the south. Dudley B. Bonsal, a senior federal judge and a Bedford resident, remembers that from the porch of his father's farmhouse he could look east and see the fishman coming over from Stamford long before he had crossed the Connecticut border. The visibility from the same site today is about fifty yards.

By 1880 the curtain was already falling on agriculture, and the trees began returning to the stage. Each shift in the economy, as people in Westchester became more dependent on the products of industry and less on those of their own land, was marked by a resurgence of woodland. Some of the trees arose when farming was abandoned. Others sprang up when coal replaced wood for heating houses and fueling locomotives. Then the charcoal industry collapsed. It had eaten up a lot of wood; for a while trees had been vital for smelting and blacksmithing. But with the adoption of fossil fuel, new stands of trees were born in Westchester.

The most important event, though, was the arrival of the car. Fields that had been kept open to pasture horses long after the demise of farming were let go when the car came. Harry Barbey brought the first car to upper Westchester in 1905. It was an open Model-T Ford which, of course, had to be cranked. Christina Rainsford, a poet from Katonah of Judge Bonsal's vintage, rode in it when she was about ten. "My mother wasn't sure if she'd let me ride in the invention. We drove up to Cantitoe Corners and turned around and came back, going all of ten miles per hour. Whenever we met up with a horse we would have to stop, and the rider would dismount and lead his frightened animal on foot past the panting machine." The motor car had taken over by 1914, and that is the birthdate of most of the current woods in Westchester.

Today, now that the land is being used for "enjoyment," as one fifth-grader I know put it, Westchester is about eighty percent woods. Although the population in the 1970s is larger than ever before, it is possible in the north-county to walk for several days, as I have done, without having to cross more than a few roads or set eyes on more than half a dozen houses. Around Somers the woods are deep and plentiful enough to have concealed for a period of three months to a year the body of a man of about sixty who had been shot once in the side of the head with a .22-caliber bullet. A rucksack beside his badly deteriorated remains, found by children in September 1974, contained the sketches of some birds, a whiskey flask, a topographical map of the area, and a few other effects which gave no clue as to his identity. Detectives were hopeful that his dental work might give them a lead, but to date the case has not been solved.

We descended between walls of granite along a steep path which doubled as a stream after rain. The trees on the next level of the mountain were tall and in vibrant prime. The air was moist and mild. With rock blocking the north and sun pouring in from the south, it was like a greenhouse here. Clusters of honey mushrooms—golden, with warts on their caps—had sprouted beneath some of the elder hardwoods. They are delectable, parboiled to remove a slight bitterness and fried in butter. But underground the fungus was devouring the roots of the trees.

A burst of machine-gun fire, followed by a peal of maniacal laughter, rang out in the woods. PILEATED WOODPECKER! one of our party sang out. A century ago, at the peak of farming, the pileated was on the brink of extinction; now that there is a supply of big, half-dead trees to excavate, the bird is becoming fairly common. The tree this one was excavating had probably been weakened enough by honey mushrooms to have been invaded by carpenter ants, the bird's favorite food.

Lying on the leaf-strewn floor was the shell of an old log. Rock-hard and weathered silver, like barnboard, the wood had resisted decay for fifty years. It was the remains of a chestnut tree. Once chestnut trees were so common that the woods in these parts were known as the oak-chestnut forest. Their nuts were sought by squirrels, deer, turkeys, and people who roasted and sold them on sidewalks. The trees grew fast. Hundred-feet specimens were not unusual. Chestnut was used as "extract timber" for tanning leather. Its durable wood was the almost exclusive choice for telephone poles and railroad ties. But in 1890 a potent fungus, *Endothia parasitica,* had arrived in the New York area, quite possibly with a shipment of trees from China. Spreading rapidly in the metropolitan area, its windblown spores encountered no resistance from the American chestnut tree. By 1904 the epidemic had been identified at the New York Botanical Garden but due to public apathy and inaction by the New York State Legislature nothing was done about it. By 1930 the chestnuts had been wiped out of their entire range. Somehow, though, in White Plains the blight missed one tree. It stood at 279 Hamilton Avenue, beside the police station, until a few years ago, when it was taken down to make room for a parking lot.

Around the log numerous shoots with long, drooping, large-toothed leaves had sprouted from the roots of the fallen tree. Rich in tannin, the roots and shoots of chestnuts are resistant to the fungus. But when a sprout reaches about twenty feet it loses resistance. Orange pustules, the fruiting structure of *Endothia*, invariably appear on its bark, and, gridled with hollow cankers, it soon dies.

We turned the log and found a snail, a packet of slug eggs, and three worms in the rich brown earth. I picked up one of the worms and stroked it. It felt bristly, which meant that it was an Asiatic worm, and not one of the native ones. The Asiatic worm had a ring of *setae* on each segment (*setae* are hairlike bristles on the underside of the worm which enable it to get around). The native one has but two pairs of *setae* per segment. Longer and hardier, the Asiatic species has been steadily usurping the niche of our native worm since it entered Westchester by way of the Midwest twenty years ago.

The fifth-grader spotted a squirrel clinging to the side of a tree. Small, reddish gold above, with a white belly and an extensible flap of skin on either flank, it was a flying squirrel, making a rare daytime appearance. There are maybe twice as many flying squirrels in Westchester as there are gray or red squirrels, but because they're nocturnal, they're seldom seen. Realizing that he'd been seen, the squirrel leaped into a hole in the tree.

Scraggly yellow influorescences had sprouted on the witch hazels, and among these tall, wiry shrubs stood a dozen or so small trees whose coarsely toothed leaves had turned scarlet. The only scarlet leaves I had seen were on tupelos, but tupelo leaves are toothless; and the only tupelos I had seen in Westchester were in swamps—never on a mountaintop. I made a cutting of the twig and leaves and months later, after it had made the round of experts, learned that the trees were indeed tupelos—an extremely rare, coarsely dentate leaf variant. The most reasonable explanation for their presence on Cross River Mountain is that they are a tiny, stranded population from a time when the woods in

Westchester were different. About four thousand years ago the climate ameliorated and some of the southern species—sweetgums, persimmons, tupelos—crept up into Westchester. Their advance was halting and irregular, and as it became cooler again most of them disappeared except in sunny, sheltered coves where a few of the trees manage to live on.

The mountain descended in tiers, each marked by subtle changes in vegetation. We jumped a number of rushing brooks, some head west to the Hudson, others east to the Long Island Sound; Cross River Mountain is along a drainage divide. We found a white moth floundering in a deep, leaf-stained pool, sending ever-widening circles of distress. The lower we got the younger the woods, and the more they'd been tampered with. Most of the trees were making their second, third, or even fourth comeback. Hardwood root systems are irrepressible: no matter how often the stems are cut, they will keep sending up new ones. The original single bole will replace itself with a "copse" of half a dozen or so sprouts. After a time, usually before they have reached a five-inch diameter, one or two of the sprouts will take the lead, leaving the others to wither away and succumb to the attack of fungi, insects, and woodpeckers.

Westchester is in a woodland known as the Sprout Hardwoods, which is in the Oak-Hickory Zone of the Central Hardwood Forest, the woods of the populous Northeast, stretching from Boston to Washington and westward to Chicago and Tennessee. The Sprout Hardwoods are rich in species because the ranges of many northern and southern trees overlap in them. The northern limit for naturally occurring sweetgum, for example, is in Rye, where it grows with beech in a rich lowland forest that benefits from the ameliorating influence of the nearby sea. American holly and Atlantic white cedar also have their northern limits in the Sprout Hardwoods. The holly is rare and occurs only in southern Westchester but the cedar inhabits swamps as far north as Bedford. As you go north and inland, farther away from the "maritime effect," white, enameled birches make their appearance. There are scattered white birches as far south as Pound Ridge. Another common member of the New England understory, striped maple, grows in high places as far south as Chappaqua, and certain bog plants like sphagnum mosses and pitcher plants—typical of New Hampshire and Maine—also dovetail into Westchester. As a determinant of vegetation, elevation is as important as latitude: Every thousand feet up is the equivalent of two hundred miles north.

We came to some woods that must have been less than thirty years old. The floor was still grass, and there were still a few "pioneer" trees—sumac, aspen, and gray birch—the first species to come into a field that has been let go. Short-lived and sun-loving, many of the birches had already died, and their rotting stems lay wedged among the maple saplings that had begun to replace them.

The site was filled with "escapes" from other parts of the world—winged euonymus, garlic mustard, Japanese honeysuckle, European bittersweet. There are dense woods in Westchester without a native plant in them. Once in Banksville, far from any house, I came upon a thriving bamboo thicket. It was the temperate bamboo of Szechwan, which grows above the rhododendron forest. Giant pandas eat it and live in it.

Even the airways have been usurped by aliens, as we were soon reminded by the raucous cackling of several dozen starlings that had flown into an ash. They were the descendants of eighty birds released in Central Park on March 6, 1890, by a man named Eugene Schieffelin. Toward the end of his life Schieffelin, whose family liquor business is the oldest in the country, had become active in the Acclimatization Society—one of several groups which enthusiastically introduced exotic species to New York. Schieffelin had chosen as his contribution to bring in all the birds mentioned in Shakespeare, of which the starling is one. Starlings are now the most abundant bird in Westchester, even more numerous than another import from the British Isles, the English sparrow. They have outcompeted a number of native species, especially the bluebird, sending them into sharp decline. Once, in Yorktown, on a Christmas bird census for the Audubon Society, a swarm of starlings flew over, darkening the sky for several moments. An experienced birder with us calculated that there were no less than sixteen thousand birds in the swarm. Murmuration of starlings—this was a blizzard of them.

While many places in Westchester have the feeling of wildness, traffic is always within earshot; and now, as we decended along Black Brook into Honey Hollow, the whoosh of cars was very near. The woods above the hollow were steep and rocky, and several huge granite blocks had fallen on each other in such a way as to make a perfect natural shelter. Once my brother and I released a racoon at the mouth of this cave, and to thank us for its months of captivity it chased us all the way down the hill to our car.

A hundred years ago the cave was used by an itinerant hermit called the Leatherman. He was called the Leatherman because the suit he wore was made out of crudely stitched scraps of leather. It weighed approximately sixty pounds and gave off eerie squeaks whenever he moved. His hat was leather and looked like a quart-size tin can with the folded-back lid as the vizor. His shoes were also of leather, of course. They were enormous, with curled-up toes and thick wooden soles, and they weighed five pounds apiece. The leather sack he carried over his shoulder was another forty pounds. In it he kept his food, a crude hatchet, a jackknife, matches, tobacco, an assortment of small tools including an awl, and a French prayer book. To steady himself he walked with a stout, ball-handled hickory cane. The man himself was short, heavy-set, bushy of brow and broad of shoulder. His small, blue-gray eyes seldom left the ground.

The Leatherman had a special route and came only to the houses of people he liked. If you were in his good book he would turn up every thirty-four days, as regular as clockwork. You'd find him standing at your kitchen door, pointing to his mouth. He would never come in, but taking your food without a word he would sit on the steps or under a tree in the dooryard and eat. People tried to get him to say something. They dunked his head into a water trough. They tried to get him drunk. But nobody ever succeeded in loosening his tongue. There was certainly nothing wrong with his appetite, though. At one sitting he once consumed a large bowl of stew, two tins of sardines, a loaf of bread, a pound of crackers, a gill of brandy, and a bottle of beer. The housewives began to look forward to his visits. They would prepare elaborate meals ahead of time and tell their children they'd better mind or the Leatherman would get them the next time he came around. Although he had no desire for attention he attracted a lot of it. The New York *Herald Tribune* front-paged a story called "Who Is the Leatherman?" The only thing that could be said for certain was that he seemed to have something on his mind.

Whatever the weather, he covered ten miles a day, sleeping in one of the thirty-four caves he had staked out in Westchester and western Connecticut. One is in Honey Hollow, another on Bull Hill, right above the Mobil Station in Bedford Hills. His entire circuit was about three hundred and sixty miles. For thirty-two years, from 1857 to 1889, he never missed a day. He even kept it up during the terrible blizzard of '88, when the snow got to be sixteen feet deep, drifting to thirty or forty. By then he was already dying. Lip cancer was beginning to eat into the sides of his cheeks, and he could only take liquid food. He was found dead in a cave on the George Dell Farm in Mount Pleasant, near Sing Sing Prison, on Sunday, March 24, 1889, and buried under a flat stone monument at the Albany Post Road entrance to the Sparta Cemetery.

After his death a rumor began to circulate that, a few days before he died, a man from France had been looking for him. This man apparently wanted to hand him over to a vast fortune in gold. People swarmed to his caves and dug them all up but found nothing. The Leatherman inspired many other wild rumors. The truth emerged when the name Jules Bourglay was found inside the jacket of his prayer book. A local newspaper reporter checked with immigration records and learned that a man named Jules Bourglay had entered the country from Lyons, France, in 1857. The reporter communicated with Lyons and discovered that Bourglay, a woodcarver, had fallen in love with one Marguerite Lazan, the daughter of a prosperous leather merchant, and she with him. The only obstacle to their happiness was Marguerite's father, who was not pleased that his daughter had fallen in love with a peasant. But finally the strength and purity of their feeling for each other broke him down. He consented to their engagement and made Bourglay a partner in his business. Shortly after that there was a depression and the business collapsed, partly due to inexperienced Bourglay's overpurchasing. Then a fire, for which Bourglay was blamed, gutted the factory. In disgrace he fled to the New World, condemning himself to wander in the woods and to abjure forever the fellowship of man.

3 *Emeralds and Erratics*

Two hundred and thirty million years ago there was no Atlantic Ocean. Africa was right off Connecticut, and its inexorable pressure against our continent was heaving up a forty-thousand-foot mountain range, higher than any around today. But in time that whole range weathered away, and after Africa drifted away, about one hundred and sixty million years ago, only the igneous and metamorphic cores of those ancient peaks remained. They are now low, rounded knobs that seldom reached more than six hundred feet above the level of the sea. Neither heavily timbered nor affording wide-open vistas, and several hundred feet short of qualifying as mountains, they are unspectacular but subtly beautiful, like most of the scenery in Westchester.

The rock on these knobs is often exposed and it is usually either gray and white in alternating, intensely contorted bands, or plain gray, or salmon-pink. The gray-white type is the most widespread formation in the county—Fordham gneiss. It used to be sandstone, containing considerable volcanic ash known as graywacke, but the pressure of the mountains that had once been over it caused the mineral components of graywacke, the quartzes, and the micas, to metamorphose into white and gray bands. For some time these remained plastic and were deformed by all the thrusting and tilting and faulting and tectonic upheaval that the region was experiencing. Gradually, however, the rock recrystallized in the striking swirls we see today. One of the nicer side effects of the new high-speed Interstate 684, which runs from Harrison to Brewster, is the magnificent road cuts wherever a knob was blasted through. The best place to see the bands of Fordham gneiss flowing white and gray is below Exit 4, where 684 goes between the sheer hundred-foot walls of what used to be Chestnut Ridge. I stop there sometimes on a clear night just to see the creamy folds glowing in the moonlight. When I taught school I used to make an analogy between Fordham gneiss and melted vanilla-fudge ice cream, but the trouble with that is that the rock is hard enough to break a chisel. In the north of Africa today you can find graywacke with the exact same mineral constituents as Fordham gneiss—one of many indications that Westchester is part of Africa's legacy to North America.

The other two major formations in the county also have their mineral counterparts in African sedimentary rock. The plain gray rock, peppered with black specks of biotite mica and almost as ubiquitous as Fordham gneiss, is Manhattan schist. It used to be a sandy shale. Most of the stone walls in the town of Bedford are Manhattan schist.

The third kind of upland rock begins to appear around Pound Ridge and Cross River. Examine the road cuts there for pinkish dikes, several feet thick, running horizontally through the gneiss. These are intrusions of a granitic magma called Pound Ridge gneiss, which melted and thrust its way through the layers of metamorphic rock during the same period in which the Fordham gneiss was formed. Cross River Mountain, where the tupelo grows, is mostly Pound Ridge gneiss. There are high cliffs and large, broken-off blocks of it covered with crustose and foliose lichens and polypody ferns. On one part of the ridge is a large, flat slab called Dancing Rock. Farmers used to squaredance on it. From another rock, called Spy Rock, you can see southeast all the way to Long Island. Below Spy Rock is a cave whose roof is blackened with what looks like soot. Nearby is water—a small upland swamp. My brother, who has a nose for archeological sites, started digging up the bottom of the cave and found some arrowheads dating to the previous millennium. On top of the rock are some curious knobs and long straight lines running toward where the sun comes up. They look suspiciously as if they had been chiseled by the hand of man, but they are probably only weather pits or glacial scratches running along the rock's fracture lines.

Nearby, however, my brother found definite chiseling—a bear and several stars carved into a boulder. Several times a year he takes people to see the Bear Rock petroglyph. Among the current residents of Cross River Mountain are the copperheads and bobcats which den in the caves and crannies. They are met with once in a blue moon. Rock-climbing clinics are held on the larger outcrops of Pound Ridge gneiss. It is a local formation, found nowhere else in the world; only in the granitic district of Westchester. You see, the rock just seeped out of the earth there. Its salmon color is due to the presence of a mineral called leptite.

The fourth formation is called Inwood marble, but you hardly ever see it because of its relative solubility. The watersheds, valleys, swales, railroad tracks, and river parkways run along the veins of Inwood marble. It is a very strong pure white crystalline marble, metamorphosed from a cherty and dolomitic limestone. Veins of the marble run intermittently all the way from Staten Island to Vermont, differing only in grain size. In Wingdale, New York, twenty miles north of the Westchester line, the marble was quarried extensively during the forties, when magnesium was extracted from it for the war effort. After the war the quarry closed down, but there's a chance that it may reopen: With everything that goes up into space these days being coated with a heat-resistant magnesium alloy, there's a new demand for the mineral.

The marble quarries of Westchester have also fallen into disuse. Maybe you've heard of Tuckahoe marble. It came from a quarry in Tuckahoe which was active from 1824 to 1900. The sidings and structural blocks of many New York buildings built in that period were Tuckahoe marble. When structural steel replaced structural marble, the quarry went out of business.

In 1921 a man named Pasquale Lucchese opened a marble quarry on Somerfield Street in Eastchester, but he was forced to shut it down two years later because the neighbors objected to the noise of the blasting. In 1924 he reopened the old Snowflake Quarry in Thornwood, so named because of the rock's distinctive crystallinity. The quarry operated until 1973 although the Lucchese family sold their interest in it in 1938. The marble was crushed into chips for terrazzo and stucco and into a finer grade powder to be used as filler for soap, asbestos, plastic, and paint; and it was also used in chemicals. The Lucchese family still has a marble business in Tuckahoe, but now all the rock is imported.

The most bizarre and beautiful part of Westchester's bedrock geology is the phenomenon known as a pegmatite. Pegmatites are veins or dikes of an abnormally fluid molten residue which pushed itself about three hundred and sixty million years ago into the cavities and fissures in the gneiss and schist. They are rich in silica, but also have feldspar, mica, and a number of rare earth elements. "Pegma" means "fasten together" in Greek, and when the silica and the feldspar crystallized together they formed a striking rock called "graphic granite"—so named because of the sympathetic alignment of the myriad silica crystals in their feldspar matrix. The rock takes a high polish and is the most common element of most pegmatites.

The quartzes tend to congregate at the center of the dike, which is usually an uninteresting dull gray quartz, but may also have rose or smoky quartz—not likely, however, to be of gem quality. It is at the edge of the core that things really begin to happen. Here "vugs"—cavities left by gases which escaped from the original molten granitic magma—have provided optimum conditions for uninhibited crystal growth. This is where you look for emeralds, aquamarines, tourmalines, smoky topazes, and other gems.

Most of the mining in the town of Bedford took place on a high, steep hill, around which the Mianus River makes a complete loop because the rock on the hill is so hard that it had resisted all attempts to erode it. There was the Kinkel Spar Mine, operated by the construction firm of O'Brian and Kinkel. They mined it, and two other pits on the hill called the Baylis and Oliver quarries, for feldspar, out of which, "in the olden days," they used to make dishes. Crushed into powder, the feldspar was used for the glaze on China. Teams of horses used to take it over to the station at Bedford Hills, and it was shipped from there somewhere south. The mines shut down "some, some time ago, I don't remember when," according to Miss Tessa O'Brian, whose brother-in-law, John Kinkel, ran them. "At least twenty years ago." After that the refuse from the mines was used locally for road material. Fragments from the quarries were distributed around the countryside. I remember when I was very young picking up bits of rose and smoky quartz in our driveway and turning them in the light. Later I would go exploring up at the quarries themselves.

You came to the first one—the Baylis Quarry—suddenly at the top of the very steep hill and the sight of it took your breath away even further: a big lake, shaped like a T, sixty feet below you, at the bottom of sheer cliffs. A floating log which a dozen or so turtles had climbed on. I am ashamed to say I dropped rocks on the big snakes sunning on ledges far below me. I was sure they were copperheads but of course they were just water snakes. Much later I got up the courage to take a running jump off the edge of the cliff, and, legs flailing, crash down with a rebel yell into the water. It was soft and slimy, wonderfully warm and buoyant and refreshing. In recent years somebody has been pouring oil into the water to discourage swimmers.

Not far from Baylis Quarry, and part of the same pegmatite, is the smaller Oliver Quarry. It has clear, green, mineral-charged water through which you can see the outlines of a car that someone drove into it years ago, and over which several sunfish are usually finning. It's like a coliseum, the walls rising all around you and the water below, with a stand of bullrushes at the outlet. Great acoustics. Across the water is a solid wall of beautifully colored rose quartz. It was unfortunately splintered by the blasting but the deep rose, translucent wall still has a powerful effect on the beholder. I went late in the summer once with a fellow rockhound, to look for a mineral called cyrtolite which I had never heard of until I read in a book called *Guide to the Gems and Minerals of America* that it is found in Oliver Quarry. It contains uranium, yttrium, and other rare earth elements and is radioactive. It appears in the fieldspar in tetragonal, red-brown crystals.

The trouble was that red-brown is the color of pretty much the whole quarry, and we didn't know where to start looking. Shortly after our arrival we found ourselves being eaten alive by mosquitoes.

We were about to turn back when from a hidden position somewhere above us a deep, dramatic voice came echoing WELCOME. The owner of the voice soon appeared—a lanky boy of about fourteen with long, kinky hair and black sneakers. His name was Doug Turet and he lived next door to the quarry. It was his secret world but after ascertaining that we were worthy of receiving the information, he was willing to share it. With a marvelous mixture of adolescent self-consciousness and grown-up authority, he began to lecture us on what we stood before: "This is a pegmatite dike, i.e., it's something like a volcano which never had enough strength to push through the surface. It's granite blown up. You can find big slabs of white muscovite mica here, and black biotite mica. They used the mica for isinglass, from which, among other things, the windows of coal-burning stoves were made. There are also twelve-sided garnet crystals, radioactive minerals like cyrtolite (our ears pricked up at this point), uraninite (black pitchblende), uranotile (white pitchblende) and other ferromagnesian minerals; smoky, rose, and citrine quartz, some of which is asteriated, potash-feldspar, soda-lime feldspar, golden beryl and green beryl (which is emerald), aquamarine, black, green, and pink tourmaline, and yellow gummite. They mined the quartz for radio oscillators, and the rose quartz was sent to China to be carved into statues."

It was obvious that Doug could have skipped a few grades without any trouble. Only a ninth-grader, he'd already written a mineral book for young kids, and not only did he collect minerals, but he cut and polished them into cabochons on a small lapidary wheel he had at home. "Here's a piece of beryl that couldn't make up its mind whether it wanted to be green or golden, so it's a mixture," he said, his eyes having sorted through the debris of the pegmatite at our feet and found something interesting. He took out a hand lens so we could see the crystals better. "I've found amethyst here. Only one other person that I know of has done that." Then he said something in a way that startled me: "Minerals grow in size and color, even though they're not alive." I was startled because I realized that, for him, they *were* alive. We stopped thinking about the mosquitoes as he proceeded to find us an example of every rock he had named.

It may come as a surprise for most Westchesterites to learn that they have emeralds and amethysts right in their own county. There's gold and silver in these hills, too, in minute amounts. Probably even fewer have heard of the Cortlandt Complex. This is a large body of mafic rock that poured out of the earth about four hundred and thirty million years ago—early in Westchester's mountainous period—and covered an area roughly coterminous with the town of Cortlandt. Perhaps the foremost expert on the Cortlandt Complex is a woman named Frances Elwyn, who lives in an adorable old house in Croton Falls which the poet Edna St. Vincent Millay rented for two years when she was just married. My friend Kaye Anderson, a crack Westchester naturalist, had kept telling me there was one "character" who could give me an "earful" whom I just had to meet. "She's eighty-five now and doesn't get around too well. She has to use a walker. But most of the time her mind is clear as a crystal. She calls herself the great stoneface."

"I'm going to strangle you. I'm going to operate on your bark," Mrs. Elwyn shouted to her Yorkshire terrier Tina who wouldn't stop snarling at me. She had been reading a murder mystery with a plaid woolen blanket draped over her knees as we came into the living room. "They're black because they're magnesium and iron-bearing—an unusual color for mafic rock," she explained when she had found out why I'd come to see her. "People have come from Germany and gotten their PhDs on them but the people who live on them don't know anything about them. There are all sorts of ultramafic rocks in the series—peridotites, pyroxenites, gabbros, norites, grano-diorites and quartz-bearing diorites.

"On Colabaugh Road there are some abandoned emery mines. Emery and its close cousin carborundum occur there in pods and lenses and were mined during the war when the Germans had cut off other sources of the mineral. Carborundum is the second hardest mineral after diamond. They used it and the emery to manufacture emery-crete. An emery-crete floor doesn't pick up oil and you can't slip on it. The steps that go down to the lower level of Grand Central are made of it."

As we left Mrs. Elwyn gave me a box containing "Twelve Rocks of Westchester" with a label briefly describing each one. I was struck by a light brown sphere which looked like a ball of clay rolled by a child, glazed, and baked in a kiln. "That's a clay baby," Mrs. Elwyn said. "It's a concretion formed in the same way pearls do in an oyster. It must have met an obstruction—probably a piece of limestone—around which the layers of clay kept laminating. You find clay babies on Croton Point." We shook hands and as we took our leave she said, "This is a wonderful place to live if you're interested in rocks. Much more interesting than somewhere like Ohio, where the soil is so deep and all the rocks look the same."

Just the day before yesterday—in relation to the rock-forming events—were the equally monumental events of the Pleistocene Epoch. The polar icecaps have always been sensitive to climatic change, shrinking or expanding whenever it gets hotter or colder, and about a million and a half years ago the world started to get colder. Perhaps a volcano erupted and the ashes in the sky screened out the sun's rays. Whatever it was triggered a great blanket of ice which crept down from the north, covering Canada and New England and most of the great state of New York, driving out the animals and smothering the vegetation. The sea went down two hundred feet. Then it got warm again and the glacier—it is now called the Nebraska Glacier—withdrew, and the sea rose again. Three more ice ages, interspersed with interglacial warm spells, followed: the Kansas, the Illinoisian, and the Wisconsin. The last glacier started to vacate the area about seventeen thousand years ago and took five or six thousand years to leave.

Almost every Westchester landscape still bears traumatic recollection of it. The ice was a mile thick. It sheered off the soil and everything that the soil had nurtured and tore off great chunks and strips of bedrock. When it melted back, it left millions of boulders scattered everywhere to make the region even less promising. Today the ice at the poles lies quiet, just as the magma in the crust lies dormant, waiting for some tectonic activity to spew it forth.

Humankind, which proceeded to establish quite a stronghold in this bleak wasteland, only started figuring out about the glaciers two hundred years ago. What got people thinking were the boulders that littered the newly cleared fields or lay just below the surface and were the bane of every colonist's existence. Occasionally they would come upon enormous ones weighing several tons apiece, propped precariously on a ledge or wedged in some impossible position. Sometimes the boulders would be clearly of a completely different rock than the kind they were resting on. Theories sprouted in the more thoughtful farmers' mind as to how the big rocks had gotten there. In 1740 Benjamin de Witt of Philadelphia expressed doubt "that so great a variety of stone should be naturally formed in one place and of the same species of earth. They must therefore have been conveyed there by *some extraordinary means."*

Today we know that the megaliths were "erratics" carried by the moving ice to their present position, often many miles from the strata in which they were originally formed. Most of the erratics in Westchester came from the Hudson Highlands, in the counties to the immediate north. They are much older rock than the indigenous strata—a billion years old. The best known erratic in the county is the "great boulder" or "balanced rock" right off Route 16 as you enter North Salem hamlet. It stands poised on a white granite shelf overlooking the Titicus River. Five white granite prongs hold it suspended four feet from the ground. The boulder itself, however, is red granite of a composition found nowhere else in Westchester. Similar red granites are found in New Hampshire and Canada. It measures about thirty feet by fifteen feet by ten feet and is estimated to weigh sixty to sixty-five tons. It was there when the first settler of North Salem arrived. As Westchester's greatest geologic freak, it was made famous by the late Bob Ripley in his "Believe It or Not" series, and people from all over the world came to see it. George Cable, whose farmhouse stands two thousand feet away, left it to the town when he died. In the immediate vicinity, in the underlying white granite formation, are seven of the most productive wells in Westchester. One nearby well, drilled through seven feet of soil and a hundred and ten feet of granite, yields nearly nine gallons a minute.

In 1873 John Jay, the ambassador to Belgium and grandson of the famous patriarch, delivered a paper to the Westchester Historical Society in which he suggested that the Balanced Rock was actually a dolmen, that it was set there by neolithic men as the capstone of a tomb. But it is hard to take his theory seriously since it presupposes that the rock was hauled there from a distance of hundreds of miles. On the other hand, there is enough room in the chamber beneath it and the shelf to bury at least a dozen men. And furthermore, how else do you explain the *very similar* dolmens at Stonehenge, where there is no neat glacial theory for the skeptics to account for them? The dolmen theory has captured the imagination of more than one person, including the late County Historian, Allison Albee. Personally, I have given the matter some consideration, and I have a hunch that the glacier dumped the rock there, along with a heap of other debris all of which was washed into the Titicus by subsequent erosion except for the five prongs which couldn't go anywhere because they were pinned down by sixty-five tons of red granite.

Erratics may offer the strongest circumstantial evidence for the presence of a glacier in Westchester, but they are by no means the only phenomena which can be most plausibly explained this way. Everywhere you look you can see that there was abrasion, and then there was deposition. To begin on the most dramatic scale: Notice how the entire Manhattan Prong tilts downward toward the sea along a northwest-southeast axis. This was the result of abrasion and tremendous pressure. The same event has largely determined the shape of each little knob in the county. Scale your nearest knob and give it the once-over. The north side will be polished smooth and gently rolling, not much different in appearance from a sand dune. Striations may be found in the rock—long, straight, parallel cuts running in the direction of the apparent ice flow. The rock may also have been fractured in a closely grouped series of symmetrical arcs, six to fifteen inches long, like folds in an old woman's skin, with their concave sides facing "downstream" and striations possibly running through them. These crescentic fractures are called "chattermarks." The smooth and usually northern slope of a knob that has been subjected to glacial abrasion is called the windward or "stoss" side. The southern or "lee" slope is steeper, lacking the polish or the striations. Large blocks of bedrock may have been rippled or "plucked" off, to end up lying together in a crazy heap at the foot of the hill. Most of the cliffs and sharp rises in elevation occur on the southern slopes of Westchester's hills. You need only to glance at a topographic map to see that the contour lines are more crowded under the hillcrests than over them. Knobs with this "stoss" and "lee" pattern of abrasion are called *roches moutonnées* or sheepsheads.

Glacial *deposition* has also been highly important to Westchester. Most of the bedrock in the county is covered with a loose assortment of boulders, gravel, sand, clay, and soil that is glacial in origin. The soil, whose parent material was transported from Putnam County, is far more important than the bedrock in determining the ecological character of the place. All the soil associations were deposited by icewater. They have great names likes Hinckley, Agawam, Wethersfield-Lackawanna, Parsippany, Rumsey, Saco, and Unadilla. Sometimes thin bands of fine clay are found in a bed overlying coarser silt, sand, or gravel. These are "varves" which, lying in suspension during the warmer months, took longer to settle out of a glacial lake than the larger-grained sediments. The unconsolidated mixture of boulders, sand, and pebbles that most often is found in the low-level intervales is called glacial "till." Sometimes the till was deposited in an oval mound that is more elongated in the direction of the ice motion. These hills are called "drumlins." Their soil and drainage characteristics make drumlins prime locations for an apple orchard. The Haight Brothers Orchard in Croton Falls is on a drumlin.

Then there are the "kames"—smaller, conical heaps of till that funneled through a hole in the ice and collected in a stagnant place. "Eskers" are long thin ribs of debris which followed the path of a river of meltwater that ran under the glacier. Long Ridge, High Ridge, and Ponus Ridge on the Connecticut border are all eskers. "Kettle holes" were formed by immense blocks of ice which were stranded in a dark place, not to melt until many years after the glacier receded. Not too far north, near Stockbridge, Massachusetts, in a steep glen in the Berkshires, there are a few patches of ice that haven't melted *yet!* As the blocks melted, they ate out deep cavities in the rock, most of which are now filled with clear, seemingly bottomless blue-green lakes. Wampus Pond in Armonk is, I suspect, a kettle hole. It has the feeling of an isolated spot in the deep evergreen wilderness of northern New England. The rugged, shady borders of the pond support only a hemlock-beech-birch forest. At the marshy inlet a pair of hooded mergansers raised a family a few years ago—the only known nesting record in the county. Finally, there are the "moraines"—long wavering lines of debris pushed along at the edge of the glacier, growing larger and larger, and finally being left there as it retreated. Long Island is the terminal moraine of the Wisconsin Glacier.

As the ice drew back, the meltwater often collected in vast temporary lakes. The Hudson River, for example, turned into Glacial Lake Hudson for a couple of thousand years. As sediment was rushed into the Hudson huge deltas formed at the mouth of every tributary. Above the delta of the Croton River a long, decurved spit called Croton Point runs out about a mile and a half into the Hudson. This singular interruption of the Hudson's eastern shoreline is a glacial feature called a "tumbeloe."

Sometimes the glacial lakes flooded over and altered the existing drainage pattern. In some cases sedimentation blocked a whole river and turned it around, making it go back to where it had started. The Ohio, which used to empty into the Great Lakes and now runs into the Mississippi, is the most famous example of this. Locally it looks as if there was at least one case of river reversal. It seems that at one point a large body of meltwater called Glacial Lake Mianus covered much of the area around Bedford Village and Banksville. It "captured" the Mianus River, a north-flowing stream which flowed into the Stone Hill River which flowed into Beaver Dam Creek which flowed through valleys now filled with the Muscoot and New Croton reservoirs into the Croton River and thence into the Hudson. Until the reservoir dams blocked their way, pelagic eels, salmon, and shad used to run up the Croton and into the Beaver Dam to lay their eggs. Perhaps before the glacier, some of them spawned as far upstream as the Mianus. But just north of Bedford Village the glacier laid down a moraine like a great wall which stopped the Mianus in its tracks. As the glacial lake grew it captured and reversed another north-running tributary of the Stone Hill, several miles east of the Mianus, and made this river its outlet. As the glacial lake shrank, the north-flowing Mianus and the south-flowing outlet merged. This explains why the Mianus River today has a sudden change of mind when it gets to Bedford Village. It used to feed the Hudson. Now it enters the sound at Greenwich.

With a run of about thirty-seven miles and a watershed of some twenty-one square miles, the Mianus is still wild and beautiful along certain stretches. It is the river I know and love best in Westchester. Both of its sources rise in Banksville, right on the Connecticut border. The source of the West Branch is a tiny spring-fed pond in the woods off Round Hill Road, behind an estate owned by eight New York lawyers who only come out on the weekend. A full-time German gardener-caretaker keeps the place immaculate. He showed me his rich compost heap and the vegetable riot in his hothouse and the deep trenches he had dug along the driveway in which he was going to plant rosebushes. I found the little pool about ten minutes back in the woods. It was scummy and overgrown and filled with the eggs of frogs and salamanders. It emptied into a swamp above which an esker ran for several hundred yards in a perfectly straight line. At the bottom of the swamp the lawyers had dredged a big pond, which was low, fringed by twenty feet of chocolate muck. A mere trickle, the West Branch of the Mianus leaves the pond soon to join forces with the East Branch, which rises in Deluca's Pond, several miles away.

By now just a little too wide to leap across, the Mianus enters a broad flats, an "outwash plain" of the old glacier. The soil here is rich and deep, with few big stones. Here the Henker Brothers grow their famous corn, and down the road from them a strong individual by the name of Paul Casson operates the Bedford Nursery, traps the muskrat and otter that swim in the river that runs behind his house, and carves duck decoys. The river continues making its way sluggishly, in no particular hurry, past Memorial Field. You can't see the current. You can't see the bottom. It glides past the village pool where the housewives from the subdivisions sit and gossip in the summertime while their children swim, past the four tennis courts which are always busy on a weekend, and the diamonds where the little league and the men's softball league have their contests.

Back in the barnstorming days, long before I was born, there used to be an airport about where Memorial Field is now. LeRow Airport it was called. A man named LeRow started it in 1929. It was just for private flying. He'd give rides and lessons and run an occasional charter trip, if somebody wanted to go to Long Island or somewhere like that. "I don't know but the grass was cut low and a sock was flying from a pole and that was about it," an old-timer told me. The planes would come in and take off in no particular pattern. They used to have parachute jumping every Sunday. The jumpers took risks and LeRow packed them in, barking at the stands with his megaphone and getting the spectators keyed up. In 1929 a German chutist named Paul Wintermeyer fell to his death when his chute failed to open, even though it had been doubled-checked. "There was another one killed too," my informant recalled, "but I can't remember his name now. He was from Long Island." The bodies were taken to the hospital in Mount Kisco on the back of a firetruck because the nearest ambulance was at Clark's Funeral Home in Katonah. LeRow Airport closed in 1938. People objected to it. The noise

45

and all. The neighbors got together and bought it up. It was considered a nuisance.

After Memorial Field the Mianus slips under the Banksville Road and disappears in an impenetrable jungle of aquatic shrubbery for several miles. A few cardinal flowers, fiery pinwheels as deep red as garnets, grow in there. There's one break in the morass where a stone bridge belonging to an old road of which there is hardly any trace crosses the river. Below the bridge is a small but deep swimming hole into which you can jump from a platform partway up in a dead tree. Twenty years ago I pulled a foot-long shiner out of the hole. A few years ago I found a good-sized marijuana plantation there, a "tea garden," as local teenagers call it.

It was during this stretch that the river begins to swing in a leisurely clockwise arc until, when it comes back in sight several miles later, it has completely reversed its direction and is heading south toward the Sound. And as soon as it changes course, it changes character, abruptly entering the Mianus River Gorge—now a wildlife refuge and botanical preserve and Westchester's greatest natural wonder. No spot in the county is so wild-seeming and so affecting.

The last time I was over there was in the fall. Kaye Anderson was paying one of her Monday-morning visits to the local places of natural interest with a dozen or so housewives. She had no objections to my tagging along, and I always like to go in the woods with her because she knows much about them. We all met up in the parking lot and set out in a single file, Kaye, the ladies, and I, through an abandoned field above the river. The poverty grass was turning red. Most of the herbs were gone. Only the late purple asters were still out. There must have been a big move the night before, because the trees were full of migrant birds. One black birch was swarming with warblers. We made out three different kinds, very hard to tell apart in their fall plumage. Another small, green nervous bird turned out to be a ruby-crowned kinglet: The white eye-ring gave it away. What is it about black birches, I asked Kaye, that attracts warblers? I'd seen another tree loaded with them the week before. "Aphids," she explained.

To our amazement, a junco was fluttering in a distant thicket, showing the white edges of its tail. It wasn't supposed to be down here until it started getting cold. Kaye noticed a movement in the crown of a black oak. It was a red-eyed vireo with black eyes—an immature male. "Red-eyed vireos," she said, "are supposed to be one of the most numerous birds in the deciduous forest. But they stay in the canopy and you don't often see them." As we continued into a young adolescent woodland typical of the region, Kaye kept showing us things: a filbert on a beaked hazelnut that the squirrels had missed; the red berries of the false Solomon's seal; orange pustules on chestnut sprouts which had gotten the blight; the tiny yellow blossoms of witch hazel. Below us the river appeared, swollen with a recent heavy rain but clear and running amber. The steep banks were clothed with hemlock, and one of the women became excited about all the mushrooms she was finding beneath them. Her accent sounded German: Continental Europeans have none of the squeamishness about fungi that is prevalent here and in Britain. She had an excellent field guide, printed in Denmark with color plates. We could have spent all morning on the mushrooms. *Tricholoma personatum*—blewit or blue leg. *Volvaria loveiana* growing in a "troop." On a fallen trunk the orange wood-loving slime mold *locogola*. A ghostly and deadly *Amanita*—the Destroying Angel. Under a beech we came upon something I'd been wondering about for a long time: a gray smudge all over the leaves, blackening some, just as if someone had dumped a bucket of ashes there. This was the waxy secretion of the woolly aphis, which is partial to beeches and dogwood, Kay told us. And sure enough, one of the limbs was encrusted with the white insects. The bark on the trunk had antler scratches. Nearby beech drops had attached the tree's root system. Because they are parasites, they don't need chlorophyll and are golden red. The chlorophyll had already been leached out of the New York ferns that had colonized the area around the beech drops: The fronds were pale yellow and soon to die away. The path went down to the river and followed it into the gorge proper. At the entrance the walls steepened and narrowed and a formation called Bedford augen gneiss was exposed. The water fell several feet and started rushing.

I let the ladies go on and watched them working their way up to the hemlock cathedral, where the trees were three hundred years old and over a hundred feet high. It seemed more like Alaska than thirty-five miles north of New York City. No one had ever cut down the hemlocks because they are second-rate lumber and firewood, that throw out sparks when burning. They hadn't been worth the trouble, and the land they were growing on was too steep and rocky to interest a farmer. In mid-April black rat snakes emerge from their dens and late in the morning you can sometimes see a dozen or so of them basking twenty to thirty feet up in the hemlocks, getting the most out of the southeastern exposure.

I watched the women walking beneath the trees. The movement of the wind in the disheveled boughs seemed in concert with the sound of the water.

Then I watched the rushing amber liquor slice through the rock, probably along a fault line, thought about the glacier, and tried to picture the river running in the opposite direction. Maybe that wasn't the way it had been at all. A booklet about the gorge explains: "We insignificant human beings, living tens of thousands of years after the Great Ice Age, should not be expected to reach unanimity regarding the forces of nature that created the gorge in the dim, far-distant past."

4 Some Punkins

Only a handful in this county of almost a million souls extract their living from the soil. Many, of course, grow vegetables in the backyard. A number of estate people play at being farmers, hiring a few hands to drive around in tractors and lend an agricultural atmosphere. But there are at least four serious vegetable farms and as many dairy farms, a few orchards (one of which, Stuart's Fruit Farm in Granite Springs, has been continuous since 1828), and a couple of poultry farms. The people who run them tend to be third-, fourth-, even sixth-generation Westchester. Many of them are kin in one way or another, and together they form the small relict population of truly rural people in Westchester.

Howland Adams of South Salem was one of them. "Born here seventy-seven years ago last Toozdy," he told me when I dropped in one evening several months before he died to see if he was interested in my old chainsaw. "My grandfather was ninety-five when he died and he'd lived here all his life. My father was eighty-seven when he died and *he'd* lived here all his life. We all lived within three miles of each other." He was sitting in one of those heavy oak Mission rockers that were popular in the rural home of about fifty years ago. Lace doilies had been draped over the arms.

49

The latest issue of *Hoard's Dairyman* was on the kitchen table. One of the light switches was enshrined with the words GOD BLESS OUR HOME. And a board on which the word KWITYER-BELLYAIKEN had been stenciled was screwed to the cellar door. Two ceramic plaques bearing scriptural homilies hung on the wall next to a Glenwood parlor wood stove whose function had been purely ornamental for a number of years now. Howland was taking in the news, seeing the damage that Hurricane Fifi had done that day in Honduras. His green work pants were held up by a pair of red police suspenders, and over a matching green work shirt he had another blue-and-yellow checked one out in whose left breast pocket was a five-pack of White Owl demi-tip cigars. A pair of horn-rimmed glasses was perched on his large hawklike nose, and the eyebrows above them were bushy and active.

His voice was a froggy rasp that came from deep down in his throat. It must have taken two thousand boxes of cigars to get it to sound like that. "I'm just getting over having my belly sewed up," he said. "Hernia. If I told you how I got it you wouldn't hardly believe it. Sneezing."

His eyes discovered the saw at my side. "Homelite, eh? How long's the rail? Most of mine are twenty-one inch. Seventeen drive links. I got one I picked up the other day. A Remington. A heavy one, goddamn good compression. She needed a diaphragm. I paid five for it." He thought for a moment. "I got three Homelites, two Wrights, a Stihl, and a McCullough besides the Remington. Know how I clean the rails? With the can opener on my jackknife." Then, out of the blue, maybe as a way of sizing me up, he popped me a riddle: "How come mice have such small balls?"

I thought it over but couldn't come close to an answer. "Beats me, Howland. How come they have such small balls?"

"Cuz only ten percent of them can dance," he said, scrutinizing me with a shrewd squint to see if I'd gotten it. Finally it dawned on me, and we both laughed. The ice broken, we then went down to his cellar to feed his beagles and look at his ax handles. Howland's ax handles were twenty-eight inches long. He had to order them specially from Maine. "You go to the store to get an ax handle today. Thirty-six inches. Christ, you'd be cutting wood in the next county." He picked up one of his to show me. "I don't know if they're hickory or ash. But the grain is in 'em good." Nearby was a box full of rusty old axheads he'd found in the woods.

"The people don't know how to hang an ax on a handle so they break the handle and throw the whole ax away."

Resting on the ax-head were three other wooden handles, too large and straight to be for axes. "The twenty-ninth of August United Parcel came in here with these three peevee handles," Howland explained, "three years after I'd ordered them." Several peach baskets full of potatoes and apples which rats had gotten into and a fifteen-gallon crock of salt pork were lying in the dirt.

The fieldstone walls of the cellar also sheltered two or three refrigerators, a honey-extractor, a number of hand mowers. Masses of cobwebs had gathered on the beams. "I could show you pictures of things we used to use that today they wouldn't know what to do with 'em," Howland said as we started back up the stairs.

"My dad was a cattle dealer and he did some real estate on the side. He sent me to Ridgfield Boys' School. I got kicked out in the tenth grade, and that was the end of my schooling. I used to sell eggs to the rich kids and lend money to them. They'd get forty dollars a week and be broke all the time. I had one guy's fur coat and he wanted it to go home to St. Paul, Minnesota, for Easter. But I wouldn't give it back to him. It was collateral. He owed me forty dollars. So, Jesus, they had me on the carpet. The principal called me in and said, I'm gonna suspend you, and I said don't bother, I won't be back. I just didn't fit in. That was the week of the *Titanic* that hit the iceberg.

"So I worked on the state road for a while. There was eight of us. Christ, we worked all day. We didn't have no trouble getting to sleep. Radio? Television? Nobody had time to listen to them things. Wintertime a couple of us got together and we filled icehouses and cut wood. Not many of us is left from those days. Chester Mead is shot in the head. Les Bowton is eighty-six on Stuart Road."

Howland had "a little wood business" cutting and delivering firewood. His son Harvey operates a dairy on the same property, and his grandson Chucky has probably the most productive pumpkin patch in the county.

"I sell about a hundred cord of firewood a year. I got six chainsaws that run good and a lickety splitter (a hydraulic splitter). I split two, three days. Then I draw it two, three days. I got eighty-six customers, I think. I must be doing something right. I deliver it split uniform and stacked for fifty-plus. Last job I did before this hernia operation I took down seventy-some trees. They were nice hickories. They ran up goddam high, sixty, seventy feet. The gypsy moths killed 'em. I took 'em down for two and a half apiece. Got forty-fifty cord.

"My son milks about forty head. Holsteins. I used to have Guernseys but then, goddammit, they don't want to buy rich milk. Harvey has one guy helping him—a half-wit. He don't do a hell of a lot. He can't. They milk 'em twice a day, seven a.m. and seven p.m. They have a pipeline milker, which helps. Twice a week a big stainless-steel tanker comes and picks up about a ton of milk and takes it to Sealtest in Meriden, Connecticut.

"We must have twenty, twenty-five acres in field corn. We use Dekall's ninety-day corn. It's all hybrid. We grow it for silage. But the goddam blackbirds they get the corn when it's in the milk (before the kernels get hard). Upstate they scare 'em away with propane guns. The neighbors here wouldn't let you get away with it.

"But I don't see how we can stay here, what with the taxes. We got sixty acres. Christ, could you get up six thousand dollars? The hell you could. I got twenty-six acres on Post Office Road I got down in 1934. The taxes were thirty-eight dollars and now they're three thousand. I tell you this place is turning into the asshole of creation, it's getting so populated. You know if I was young I think I'd go to Australia."

It was another hour before Howland got around to making an offer for the saw. We haggled a bit, and I finally let him have it for ten dollars.

A while later I heard that Howland had been telling people about this real sucker he'd taken to the cleaners. He was sure the saw was worth at least twenty.

Besides being a shrewd dealer in used chainsaws Howland was also the dog warden for the town of Lewisboro. As he put it, "I pick up dogs and bitches." Too old to run after a dog, he would just squat down and call it to him. One time he had to go over to the Seeligs and catch the bees that had gotten into their cellar. George and Ellen Seelig live a few miles to the south on the Ward Pound Ridge Reservation, the forty-five-hundred-acre county park where George has been employed as an outdoor maintenance man for the last twenty-six years. He's the only man on the reservation who knows how to drain the water pipes before the ground freezes. He's sixty-three now, a short, earnest man whose eyes are large and trusting behind his powerful glasses. Ellen, fifty, is more earthy, and speaks in a strong, husky voice. She was born in Honey Hollow, three miles away. One night when I dropped in she handed me a drink with a swizzle stick on top of which a pair of pink plastic gambs were thrashing. "Bottoms up," she said.

George met Ellen when she was twelve. He had stopped by to see her older sisters, but he ended up waiting for her to grow up. "Still waiting," George Jr. interjected. He was seventeen and bearded, mainly interested in vehicles.

They were married in 1944, after he'd gotten back from North Africa. He was wearing the uniform of the 591st Engineers, and they drove off in a Chevrolet with a sign on the back that said, "Just Married (ye gods)," to honeymoon with his brother in Lennox, Massachusetts. He came to work at the reservation in 1949, after working for a year on the town roads. Bill Whitman, the superintendent, hired him. "It was Howland Adams who got me the job. He told Pa Whitman he'd be missing out on a good man if he didn't hire me. Pa Whitman asked me what I could do. I said name something and I'll tell you if I can do it. He said hand mowing (with a scythe), chopping wood, crosscut sawing, and I said I could do all those things. We only got chainsaws on the reservation fifteen years ago. Pa Whitman would make a trip around three times a day to make sure you were doing an eight-hour day. It wasn't four hours like today. He was a good man. He walked with authority."

On Memorial Day the Seeligs plant their enormous garden: potatoes, onions, carrots, beets, Swiss chard, beans, cucumbers, cauliflower, broccoli, peppers, eggplant, red and white cabbage, lettuce, radishes, tomatoes, zucchini, Brussels sprouts, okra, acorn and butternut squash, corn, large "punkins" for jack-o'-lanterns, little sugar punkins for pies. "As fast as the garden grows, my wife is putting down and laying up," George told me. "I put three hours in the garden after work just to rest up."

"I used to can in mason jars but now you just cook 'em up a little bit and throw it into the freezer," Ellen explained. The Seeligs buy their meat by the front quarter and get it all cut up into chuck steak, pot roast, and stew meat. They have a Franklin stove stuck in the living-room fireplace and a two-burner wood stove in the kitchen to supplement the oil furnace which replaced their two wood stoves in 1953. In the fall they put in about seven cords of deadwood—mostly hickory and hard maple—which George picks up on the trails. By the time winter comes they've laid up their food and fuel; they're so well provisioned they wouldn't even have to leave the house.

Being in the middle of a huge park the Seeligs enjoy a variety of wildlife: Deer come right into the dooryard, and every spring a pair of wrens move into the birdhouse on the front lawn. Below the house is one of the few regular nesting sites for bluebirds in the county. "We used to have orioles steady every year in the first tree out here. The kids used to throw out string for them to build their nests with," Ellen said. "But I haven't seen them in the last two years."

"There used to be a lot of fox on the reservation, too," George told me. "Their favorite food was the stray cats. Every fall there's always at least fifteen cats left at the dump before the snow flies. But the mange has killed the foxes off. The last one I saw was five years ago. It was completely lacking hair except for a little bit on its ears and on the tip of its tail."

As I left George took me down to the cellar where he had set his pumpkins. A few days before, the first frost had nipped the vines, and he told me to take my pick of the twenty or so gourds that were sitting in the dirt. I picked out an unblemished, well-shaped, medium-sized one, but George insisted that I take the biggest one of the lot—about a sixty-pounder.

"So what do you want to know?" I had waded through a sea of beets to get to Franz Henker, who was stooped over, pulling up the bigger plants, tying them up in bundles, and throwing them to one side, where he could pick them up on the way back. It was obvious that he was not going to stop working and that if I wanted to talk with him I'd have to follow him up and down the rows. "Frank, they call me," he said through teeth that were clenching a Tiparillo. Frank and his brother Ernie have the only entirely self-sufficient vegetable farm in the county, on the road to Banksville. "The others they all grow a little, buy the rest. We don't buy anything. Just like today, we're out of lettuce. When we're out, we're out. We're strictly fresh every day." The reputation of Henker's sweet corn is unsurpassed in the region.

Their father had come from Austria in 1917. "We farmed in White Plains before we come up here. My father bought this in 1937. We built the house, the garage, and the barn. We have twenty-three acres and a fraction. Eighteen, twenty are farmed. We have all kinds of vegetables. We rent the next-door neighbor's fields and thirty-five acres from IBM in Armonk. We grow beets, acorn, butternut, zucchini, and summer squash, peppers, corn, tomatoes, lettuce, pumpkins, kohlrabi, radishes. The soil is good. We keep feeding it all the time.

"We start out at six o'clock picking corn. That's the first thing we do is pick corn. We hire five or six kids to help pick in the summertime. They work eight to five. We're out there all day, seven days a week, no days off. If it gets bad weather we put on our raincoats. We start third week of March. Quit Halloween. In winter we clean up the whole place, seed a cover crop (rye), spread manure, take it a little easy, and before you know it it's the third week of March.

"The reason there are no other farms here is that it's too expensive to start out now. And all the good vegetable land is golf course or got houses on it. Only rock piles left." I asked him what kept him farming. "I guess we're farmers because it's all we ever did. Too late to quit now. We're over sixty. We'll keep farming till one of us drops dead, I guess."

Just then his sister-in-law Helen's voice came from the shed, in front of which a constant stream of ranch wagons was pulling in and out. "Frank, it's quarter past five and I'm down to three bags." So he planted a broom handle at the last beet he'd yanked up, lit up another Tiparillo, and started walking toward the shed to bring her some more corn.

Ernie was spraying copper over a patch of tomatoes several fields in the distance. He's a year younger than Frank but looks a bit older. The family resemblance is strong. "No use bothering me, 'cause I'm hard of hearing and I couldn't understand you while I got this machine going and I got three more rows to go," he yelled. So I waited for him to finish and watched the killdeer skimming the open ground. When he shut off the machine I could hear the birds screaming. "Look at these tomatoes," Ernie said. "The vines are three-quarters gone. I wouldn't be wasting this fungicide on them except I had some left in the tank. What with the humidity and heat wave we've had we couldn't keep the lot clean. It's a question of weeds and mud. Every year there's something that bothers you. One year the insects will eat you out of house and home. One year'll be too dry, the next too wet. I like a dry year myself.

"Timing is the important thing in this work. If you can't do it on time then it takes longer and costs you two or three times more or else you just disk it up. Right now the deer are a terrible problem: They eat green tomatoes, pull the carrots out of the ground, and destroy the corn. They eat the tassle as it comes out of the whirl so you don't get pollination. There were five big bucks in the orchard this morning with racks like this [shows]. Who's got the time to watch them?" Not Ernie. Every couple of years he takes a week off and goes icefishing on Lake Champlain. That's the only vacation he allows himself.

"The future doesn't look good. All the government agencies are making it hard for us. Birds are our biggest pest. Blackbirds and starlings. Aphids, leafhoppers, and of course flea beetles are a problem. We're in it because of the investment we got in it and we're in our sixties and what would we do till we retire? When one of us can't do it anymore we'll probably quit. We're so used to it, it doesn't bother us. It's like getting up and eating."

Ernie looked up at a Cooper's hawk which was flapping against a densely wooded hillside. "That used to be Bald Hill," he said. "This was dairy country around 1900. This was the milkshed of New York." I speculated aloud that a glacier must have had something to do with the creation of this rich plain, an unusually broad and level tract for the New England Uplands, probably a basin in which the icewater collected and unloaded its sediments. "Don't ask me about no glacier," Ernie said. "I haven't been here that long. But this is ideal vegetable ground. All we need is somebody to do the work."

At the corner of Wood and Croton Lake roads in Mount Kisco two men were sitting at a table. An old green pickup was parked a few feet away and there was a sign in front of them which said, SWEET CORN $1.20 DOZ. Below them was a big field in which several dozen Canada geese were grazing, and at the bottom of the field a cow pond half hidden by foliage.

56

Business was slow. Rain had been misting' down all afternoon, and the two men were playing dominoes. One of them was old and ruddy-faced and clearly worked outside. His name was Harry and the eye of a peacock feather was stuck in his hatband. The other man was twenty. He had a red beard, black Wellington boots, green pants, a khaki shirt, and wore a folding knife on his belt. His name was Steve Wood.

Steve is the sixth generation of Woods to have lived and farmed on this spot. The Woods settled it in 1803, having come to Bedford a few years earlier from England via Long Island. It was Steve's great-great-grandmother and namesake Stephen Wood who gave Mount Kisco its name. The Woods are Quakers. A little way from their homestead is a meetinghouse where they have worshiped for a century and a half. Their house sits on a rise and can be glimpsed from the road through a grove of magnificently aging ornamental trees. It is impressive: sided with rough-hewn granite blocks quarried locally, with white shutters and a green mansard roof surmounted by an array of clay chimney pots. The third house on the spot, it was built in 1873 and is called Braewold. "There was a huge wave of Irish immigrants at that time who were willing to work for practically nothing, so conditions were good for building a big house," Steve's mother, whose name is Twinkie, told me. A large Victorian porch faces the valley, and on the other side one enters the kitchen through a screen porch under an enormous set of caribou antlers. Peacocks and white and gray guinea hens, a traditional feature of the Woodpile, as friends call the homestead, patrolled the courtyard possessively. One was walking across the stone arch, smothered with an orange-blossomed trumpet creeper, which spans the house and a tall garden wall which is in turn connected to the stone carriage house.

A single, elegant corn plant with a few kernels beginning to swell on it was growing in the courtyard. Boulders of rose quartz and a large granite slab balanced on four garnet-encrusted stone legs attested to James Wood's (Steve's great-grandfather's) fascination with local minerals. The sense of place in this courtyard was strong and quite un-American, more like an ancestral seat somewhere in the English countryside. As far as I could determine, this has been the longest tenure of a piece of property in the county.

The reason why the Woods have been able to remain here for so long is that four generations ago, as farmers were beginning to go under, the family took up other occupations: Stephen, the first Wood to inhabit Braewold, became a blacksmith-farmer; his son James was a gentleman-farmer who served on the boards of several colleges and wrote articles on agriculture and education (his writings about Westchester County are by far the most readable and informative that I have come across). James's son Hollingsworth was a lawyer-farmer who practiced in the city, and *his* son James is a New York bank vice-president—farmer. "The love of farming has passed down but it has not been self-supporting for several years," Twinkie explained.

Going back to the land that his family never left, Steve is the first Wood to be a full-time farmer since Stephen, more than a hundred years ago. He was majoring in animal husbandry upstate at Cobleskill Agricultural and Technical College. "I'm studying beef," he said. "How to raise them as calves and sell 'em as hamburger." On weekends and in the summertime he came down to run the farm. A few days later I found him in a pasture going over feeding systems with a salesman from Oneida. They were discussing the virtues of various models of feed mixers and conveyor belts to carry the feed in and out of a silo that Steve was fixing to build. One of the Woods' forty-five Herefords was standing nearby, yanking up the grass and masticating it vigorously. At the end of the summer the cattle would be quartered and frozen in a slaughterhouse in Yorktown. Besides the cows there was an assortment of flat-bed trailers, some with sidepanels and some without, and an apparently disused hayrack through whose palings a variety of weeds—burdock, lamb's-quarters, greater and lesser ragwort—were growing. In an old, weathered shed up on stone blocks was a foot-powered corn husker; the shucked corn went down a wooden sluice and out through the side of the shed. The farm is two hundred and seventy-five acres in all. Fifteen were in field corn this year, seven in sweet corn, fifty-five in hay (a combination of timothy, alfalfa, trefoil, and orchard grass), fifty in pasture, and the rest in woods. As they were talking, Steve packed a wad of Day's Work tobacco into his cheek and began kneading it with his teeth into a succulent chaw, sluicing off the excess juice from time to time into the grass.

I asked Steve what had attracted him to farming and he said, "Being your own boss. Setting your own hours. Being free. Of

58

course you have some commitments, but not like a nine-to-five job. And it's what I enjoy. Just working outside."

On a sharp bend of Route 22 five miles north of Armonk, the tiny settlement of Coman Hills is easily overlooked. The only people who stop are friends of Elsie Ferris and her daughter Muriel. At its height it boasted a one-room schoolhouse, a Socony gas station, and a blacksmith shop that served the surrounding estates. But it never rated a church, a saloon, or a post office. It never got to be a hamlet; there just wasn't any room for Coman Hills to grow in its little rocky hollow. Probably the best word for it is a "corners" because a road *does* run into it a hundred yards from the bend. Alice Joyce, who is married to the chief of the Mount Kisco Fire Department, grew up there thirty years ago.

Alice was christened Bliss Freelove, but the kids in school teased her about it, so she took her grandmother's name. "The school had eight grades and one teacher," she recalled. "I used to sit on a board in the old pine tree and do my homework. We had outdoor plumbing. It was out in the garage. We used to be able to count the cars that went by on a Sunday: We'd sit on a boulder and wave to them as they went by and be disappointed when they didn't wave back. It was mostly the Colonial sand truck and the Greyhound bus and that was about it."

Alice's Aunt Elsie lives in the little brown-shingled house with a screen porch right on the road. I remember driving by the house as a child because it had an extremely tall brick chimney braced from every direction with metal rods. But the chimney was knocked over several years ago in a windstorm. I had never been in the house or even heard of Coman Hills—though I grew up only five miles away—until Alice Joyce took me to see Elsie and Muriel one afternoon.

The two women were sitting on the screen porch in sun-deck chairs. A towel with a map of Florida was draped over the back of one of the chairs. As Elsie Ferris and I shook hands a motorcycle whizzed by. "That's nothing," Elsie said. "We saw nineteen go by here Sunday. We counted the cars for an hour. Just one way was a hundred and four cars. And trucks! We have an awful lot of trucks by here. We had a beer truck and a truck of chickens overturn on the bend. Chickens was all over the place. And

59

LISTEN, I'll tell you what else we had: EGGS." Elsie must have been well into her eighties, with her creamy white hair done in a coronet and tucked under a hairnet, her gold-rimmed spectacles, her terrycloth apron over a cotton print shirtwaist dress, her stockings and blue "sneaks." I asked her if she minded revealing her age.

"Don't mind a bit. It's just that I don't know myself," she said, laughing heartily.

"Every birthday she says she was seventy-nine," Muriel explained. "But she can't be seventy-nine *every* birthday." Muriel was a slight, shy, gray-haired woman dressed in slacks and a flowery blouse.

"I guess I was born in 1894. I was born Elsie Marie Agor. My father was a farmer in Mahopac. We had everything: cows, horses, potatoes, corn. I married Howard Camman Ferris in 1918. We moved to Coman Hills when our boy Sonny was four years old. The house was all brand-new lumber and everything. We paid rent for it for the time being. Howard worked on the road. Maintenance man, you'd call him. He put in the iron post fence just before the bend and painted the center line by hand. Then he started running a Socony gas station, too." In front of the house were some mounds in the driveway where the pumps must have been. "He died in 1949 but I ran it till 1955 when we got hold-up men, then I gave it up."

Next door, hidden by tremendous overgrowth, is the small, brown-shingle house where Alice grew up. Elsie's brother-in-law Clinton Ferris lives in it now. "It was a beautiful house but my Uncle Clinton let it go to wrack and ruin." Elsie and Clinton have not spoken to each other in twenty-some years. "But Aunt Elsie kind of likes it," Alice told me. "It keeps her going."

The farthest away Muriel had ever been from Coman Hills was to Mount Kisco or Armonk to get something at the store or to take in a movie. Now at the age of sixty she was going away for the first time, with Sonny and his family, who live in New Rochelle, to the motel overlooking Lake Winnipesaukee in New Hampshire where they usually go every summer. "I'm homesick already," she confessed. "Four days will go quick though, I bet." She fell silent, and in the lull between cars the cicadas started up, quietly at first but pretty soon every cicada in Coman Hills joined in the chorus until their collective drone in the hollow was almost deafening.

The Bedford Farmers' Club is the oldest organization in the county that's still going and possibly the oldest organization of its kind in the country. It was founded in 1851 for "the improvement of agriculture and the sciences" after Arnall F. Dickinson's ailing horse had died in spite, or conceivably because, of the attempts to make it well. Dickinson had started by administering six bottles of "strong sage tea, sweetened with molasses, mixed with a little turpentine and spirits." Then, Dickinson recounted, "Jared Powell urged ginger tea, and with but little faith myself, gave him a bottle of that. And then Horrace Miller happening along suggested and we all consented to about a pint of strong physic, bleeding, and injection of a decoction of tobbaco sweetened with molasses—to which, as a last resort, I consented and the applications were made. The physic given was three-fourths of a pound of Epsom salts and nearly a bottle of lard." After a few more administerings of an "Aloetic Ball" which he describes as consisting of "ten drachms of aloes mixed with molasses and a little turpentine," the horse died.

While the meetings of the Farmers' Club have now more historical than practical value, they are still held regularly. Crackers and cheese, tea, coffee, and fruits in their season are served. At one meeting, years ago, a stick of oleomargarine was placed among thirty sticks of butter, and even the members of the club who were most outspoken against the new product couldn't tell which one it was. At another meeting the pros and cons of a new fertilizer called "superphosphate of lime" were debated. In the September meetings the farmers usually bring the pick of their crops and engage in a little friendly competition. At the last meeting it was Harry Buford's twelve-foot-four sunflowers that stole the show.

The 122nd Annual Meeting took place in October at the home of Mrs. Wilhelmina Waller. Mrs. Waller raises thoroughbred horses and lives in a large Victorian house on Guard Hill. On the porch were some of the biggest pumpkins I'd ever seen. "Some pumpkins they got on the front porch there," an old man sitting in the fold-up chair next to me observed.

According to the seventh edition of Ripley's *Believe It or Not*, the world's largest pumpkin was grown in Mount Kisco in 1918. It weighed a hundred and sixty-five pounds and was nine feet around. The foremost pumpkin grower at the moment is Howland Adams's sixteen-year-old grandson Chucky, who raises them semiprofessionally and consistently produces whoppers. His secret is "a lot of manure and clipping off some of the other pumpkins so all the strength goes to one." Chucky raises Big Macs. "They don't have good color but they're big. They start off yellow then turn pink."

A few of Mrs. Waller's pumpkins were right up there in the hundred-pound category. "When Mrs. Waller tells those pumpkins to grow, they grow," her personal secretary told me proudly. And Mrs. Waller herself explained, "Those are Big Macs. They just wouldn't stop growing. They always seem to get that big. Maybe that's all they're good for."

Everyone took their seats and the president called the meeting to order. Mrs. Waller, who is on the board of several national conservation groups, reported that the loss of farmland to urban sprawl and residential expansion in the United States was now at 1.4 million acres a year. She also said that hardware disease in cattle, caused by people chucking pull-off can tops into pastures, was up fifteen percent. Then the secretary gave a report on the older members who had gone to nursing homes, how they were doing and how they could be reached. Most of the people in the club are over sixty. Then someone got up and said, "The woolly bears and the *Farmer's Almanac* tell us we're in for a hard winter." (As it turned out they were both wrong.) The historian gave a résumé of what had happened at the meeting a hundred years before and someone else in the course of a rambling reminiscence came out with the saying, "Even if a farmer intends to loaf, he gets up in time to get an early start," which everyone thought was a pretty good one.

Up in the front row, because he was hard of hearing, was William H. Saunders. He had served for forty-one of his ninety-four years as secretary of the club. Early in his life he had gained a wide reputation as a breeder of Guernseys, rearing two world-champion butter-producers. Later on he kept busy with his many hobbies, one of which was the painting of rural scenes on the undersides of shelf fungi. He was also a taxidermist. In our nature museum we have a red fox, a weasel, a red squirrel, and several perching birds which were found dead on the road, stuffed, and mounted by "Pop" Saunders. Most remarkable of all is the great blue heron that hangs from the ceiling, with its wings fully extended, which was found in a marsh one February morning standing dead with its legs frozen in ice, and taken to him. Beyond that Mr. Saunders was a woodworker who designed and made chairs and cabinets as well as miniature rooms furnished from different periods in American history. He was also a humorist whose witty observations had enlivened the *Farmer's Almanac*. He liked to reminisce but made it plain he had no desire to relive the past. "The good old days were pretty horrible in my opinion," he told a reporter from the local paper when he turned ninety. "In my boyhood they didn't know what appendicitis was and people used to die of it. There was plenty of smallpox and diphtheria too." He pointed out that people "used to have about a ten-mile radius. Now you can go out in wider circles, see more people, get wider ideas." One of his favorite sayings was "the time to do it is not before, not after, but now." I knew all about him, although I had never been introduced to the long-jowled sage.

And before I had gotten the chance to meet him, I heard he was in the hospital, dying. Then a few days later word came that he was dead, and I could only think of the truth of his saying, of how I had put off going to see him, and now it was too late.

Of the people who had come to pay their last respects to Pop Saunders at the Clark Funeral Home that Thursday in Katonah, many had canes and white hair. The casket was open at the end of the room, and you could see his huge embalmed profile above the rim: the large, noble nose with its sweeping curve like the stem of a pipe going down to the bowl, the immense nostrils, the down-turned mouth.

People were going up to take a last look at him, and those who were Catholic were kneeling on a cushion in front of the casket and crossing themselves, and the most bereaved friends and next-of-kin were sitting in the front row in a sofa, hugging each other. Behind me I could hear two women commenting on the flowers and naming the people as they came in. The flowers were mostly gladiolas. The Bedford Hills Fire Department had sent a large bouquet. My brother had sent a bunch of wildflowers in behalf of his nature museum. "I don't see many young," one of the women said.

63

"That's the Shoumatoff boy, isn't it?"

"Where'd he get his height from?" I turned around and bowed politely.

"Hush now. There's the minister." A kind-looking young man in a gray suit and a white collar, with bushy eyebrows and a benevolent smile, walked up confidently to the lectern and flicked on the light. "The number of people here today," he began, "attests to the knowledge, care, concern, yes, even the love of Mr. Saunders." He spoke first about Mr. Saunders, who had been "one great individual, one who has been well acquainted with the greenery and the gardens of Bedford for lo, these several years." Then he spoke for a while about "that existence called heaven—I won't say place," where the man had gone. "We must not think of heaven as an endless row of houses, suburban or brownstone." He spoke well and just long enough, but perhaps a bit too softly, for one of the ladies behind me kept whispering, "I can't hear. Can you hear?"

5 The View from Brookside

Just east of Mount Kisco the road becomes straight. As telephone poles flicker by, you pass a wooded swamp on the right, then a small, brown-shingled cottage—an old house from the rural period—smack on the road, behind a stone wall and a latticed fence. Several feet from the road the wild divisions of a great white pine reach high above the roof and the surrounding forest. The tree must be three hundred years old. Fifty years ago the plan to blacktop the rutted country lane out front called for the big pine to be cut down, but when the pavers crew came, a strikingly attractive woman stepped out of the cottage, threw her arms around the boss of the crew, and begged him to let the tree live. Because of this "tearful interview," it is still there.

A little way up from the big pine a noisy brook runs under the road, purls along behind the cottage, tumbles over two small waterfalls and under six stone footbridges built at the turn of the century and finally oozes out into the swamp. A few trout stand in the shadows below the footbridges; small minnows called dace dart around in the pools; milk snakes and black snakes lie coiled on overhanging branches; dusky and two-lined salamanders rest between rocks. Half a mile later the brook joins the Kisco River, which loops around Mount Kisco, then heads for the New Croton Reservoir. From there some of the water is piped down to the people of New York City, some released into the Hudson, and some evaporates. As far as we know, the brook has no name. The cottage is known as Brookside.

It was built around 1830 and has the small, low rooms, steep stairs, and central chimney typical of the rural wood-heated structures of its day. Its first occupants were a shoemaker named Finch—Alexander Finch—and his wife, Charity. They had three sons, Frank, William, and James, the last of whom blew out his brains when he was twenty-eight in what is now the dining room.

Charity outlived her husband by several decades and was often seen around the turn of the century—a crippled old woman by then—sitting on the piazza while her grandchildren played at the ford. After she died the cottage housed a junk dealer named Homer Piersall and his collection. Then, in 1905, leaning crazily over the brook and in the advanced stages of dilapidation, it fell into the hands of the strikingly attractive woman whose name was Martha Leonard.

Miss Leonard was the restless daughter of a retired colonel who lived on a nearby hill. At sixteen, she had run away. Two years later, the private detective her father had hired to find her finally tracked her down in London, where she was studying to be an actress. She agreed to come home, and shortly afterward became involved with a young man who did not meet with her parents' approval. So they sent her back to Europe on an ocean liner, this time in the company of an elderly chaperone. After several days at sea, however, her lover showed up on deck. He had stowed away, much to the dismay of the chaperone. Miss Leonard did not return to Mount Kisco for twenty years. When she did, she was in her late thirties, and wanted a place of her own. Remembering the old widow who had fed her doughnuts as a child and told her stories on the front stoop, she settled in "the old Charity place."

Her first step was to have the cottage jacked up and resilled, painted without and whitewashed within. By slow degrees she converted Charity's dooryard into an elaborate garden with a sundial, a network of secret paths, and a profusion of flowers grown from cuttings which she had begged, borrowed, or stolen. When a freak tornado hit Westchester in 1907, knocking down the chestnut trees (already weakened by the blight) in the surrounding woods, she had the straight young ones brought out and fluted by the local turner to look like Greek columns. Five of them went to support the trellises of an arbor she built off the house and hung with vines—clematis, wisteria, ampelopsis. Eight more framed the stage of an outdoor amphitheater which she opened on September 22, 1911, with a morality play called *The Treason and Death of Benedict Arnold*. The play was in iambic pentameter and had a full Greek chorus of Waves and Clouds. It starred a man with a long beard named Henry Chapman and was written by his brother, John Jay Chapman. The Chapmans were great-great-grandchildren of our first Chief Justice. Henry was Miss Leonard's admirer for many years. John was a poet whose thin volumes of verse attracted more of a following abroad. Once during a quarrel he struck a man and was so filled with remorse that recalling the scripture, "If thy hand offends thee, cut it off," he plunged his sinful limb into a fire and left it there till it was consumed.

Other plays, pantomimes, operas, and concerts were put on in the Brookside Open-Air Theatre, drawing spectators from country houses in the vicinity and from New York, which was a two-hour drive by motorcar. The audience sat on six stone tiers—men wearing white linen suits and straw boaters, the women in muslin dresses with long sleeves, high necks, and cinched waists, and wide-brimmed straw hats bedecked with flowers. Among the theatricals put on at Brookside was the first English performance of *Lysistrata*, an ancient Greek comedy about sexual politics, sponsored by the Women's Political Union in behalf of suffrage. Shaw's *Don Juan in Hell* had its American debut here. In *Pinkie and the Fairies*, society girls in diaphanous costumes danced barefoot on the grass—still a shocking idea in those days. Miss Leonard, under the name Rose la Tour, had been among the first to introduce barefoot dancing in New York. During a rehearsal for one of her outdoor barefoot ballets, the cast made the mistake of cavorting in a patch of poison ivy, and some members came down with bad cases. She kept a scrapbook of photographs, programs, clippings, and other mementos of the shows that were put on at Brookside during the ten years of its heyday. The scrapbook came with the house, along with a watercolor of phloxes in the garden. Among the famous actors pictured are Ruth St. Denis, Ben Greet, Ted Shawn, Walter Hampden, and Sir Henry Irving. A woman swears she saw Isadora Duncan at Brookside "sometime after 1915," but there is nothing in the scrapbook to corroborate it.

My favorite shot is of a man named Effingham Pinto, prostrated before two rather plump ladies named Ada Lewis and Blanche Bates, in an emotional scene from *Madame Butterfly*. Miss Leonard appeared in most of the productions as Martia Leonard, although her friends all knew her as Martha.

What apparently put an end to the amphitheater was the institution of Daylight Savings Time in 1918. Since audiences had to get back to New York it was no longer possible to schedule the performances late in the evening, when the shadows were long and cool, and Brookside was at its best, and it was too hot and humid to have them in the midafternoon. So throughout the twenties Miss Leonard operated a tea garden. The Rockefeller boys—Nelson, Laurance, Winthrop, and John—would come all the way from Pocantico Hills for her homemade bread.

At the same time, she turned to her second love, gardening. Neighbors and their children continued to use the open-air theater for an occasional production of *A Midsummer Night's Dream*, but the six stone tiers were gradually turned into flower beds, and clones of Christmas fern, clumps of moss pink, rosettes of foxglove, and colonies of columbine sprouted where the spectators had once sat. In the fertile hollow where Miss Leonard had reclaimed, *ipso manu*, just under two acres, she spent most of the next thirty growing seasons digging into the soil with her trowel to make room for the likes of hollyhocks, poppies, bachelor's buttons, sweet williams, phlox, verbena, rose campion, heliotrope, and mignonette, and providing them with the gracious shade of redbuds, rhododendrons, laurels, azaleas, and Japanese maples. She would garden in long skirts, and smocks she had embroidered herself, and when she went out she would dress up in perky flower prints. After the theater was closed, a man twenty years her junior named Robin Hamilton, who had starred in many of the productions, stayed on with her, crossing lilies and irises in a flat, open bed that faced south, and coming up with several new varieties. In 1946 Miss Leonard had a mystery novel called *The Moving Finger Writes* printed by a vanity press in Boston, and in 1957 she brought out a book called *O All Ye Green Things*, which was a summation of her gardening experience, a history of gardening in the Western world, and a manual for beginners. Both works are charming.

Brookside had become by then more than she could manage, and not being the sort of person who could bear to stand by as her garden went to seed, she sold the place for six thousand dollars to her lawyer and moved with Hamilton and her pet crow to a smaller spread around the corner called "the Canary House." The two of them would spend their days together pottering around in a less demanding garden and their evenings by a fire, reading aloud to each other from the Bard. Neither of them cared much for housekeeping, so the interior of the cottage, according to all reports, deteriorated in appearance, while the grounds became some of the loveliest in the region. Toward the end of her life, Miss Leonard became a well-known character in the village. People remember her descending on the Anne Beauty Salon in Mount Kisco to have her hair washed—dressed in a long black skirt that was on crooked and black stockings that had fallen down and flat sneakery kind of shoes and a straw pork-pie hat pushed back on her head under which the white hair shot out in every direction. And out of this strange apparition there would suddenly come a rich and cultivated voice, asking quietly but with absolute authority for Mrs. McTavey.

Miss Leonard died in 1964 at the age of ninety-three. For all but the last year, she had tended her own garden. She had wanted her ashes flown over Brookside and scattered to the wind, but there were legal complications to executing her wishes. For a year the ashes stood in an urn on her lawyer's desk while people wondered what to do with them. Finally, in a small ceremony attended by relatives, a few friends, and Hamilton, her last and longest lover, they were buried on the wooded slope overlooking the amphitheater. The stone head of a beautiful young woman, with her hair in tresses like a cameo, marks the spot.

A decade later, Miss Leonard's heritage provides us with a roof. A few years after her death, her lawyer moved out to Salt Lake City, and the house, with eighteen acres, was acquired as part of a nature sanctuary. My wife and I were offered the cottage rent free in return for tending the garden, conducting a Sunday-morning birdwalk, and maybe getting a thing or two happening in the amphitheater again.

When we moved in, the place was completely overgrown. The house had been rented to a succession of tenants—a doctor, a Canadian music teacher who practiced the Orff method, and a man who commuted to a publishing house in the city until he contracted tuberculosis. With each change of hands, the grounds had fallen into deeper neglect. The glade where Hamilton had crossed lilies and irises was now, by the end of summer, choked with goldenrod, joe-pye weed, and other invaders. I spent the first few weeks pulling up the seedlings of twelve kinds of native trees that had started in various parts of the garden. It was a lot of work, but it went easily. The garlic mustard came up willingly, as if it knew it shouldn't be there. The wisteria vine offered little resistance as I unraveled it from the big ash where it had slowly been strangling to death. Every hour was rewarded with the discovery of a new flight of moss-covered steps or a secret path, and I felt as if Miss Leonard were looking down on me, silently voicing her approval. We cleared a place for a small vegetable garden and planted it with tomatoes, lettuce, peppers, and sunflowers. By the end of September, the cultivated part of the sanctuary was under control, and I started to look around in the woods.

I found a path along the little swamp where the brook fanned out. There I discovered the biggest shadbush I'd ever seen. In the heart of the swamp, among cushions of moss and tussocks of sedge, I came across a green half-pint bottle whose contents must have been consumed by someone with a strong throwing arm, unless the bottle had been washed there by a spring flood. In time I found other cans and bottles of all sizes and shapes, including one that said, "I like my wife's salad dressing."

Between the swamp and the ridge above it was a level terrace, thinly wooded and suggestive of the time when most of Westchester was clear. The ashes, oaks and hickories there were even-aged and no more than fifty years old, dating from the time when horses were retired by "gas buggies" as the way to get around. Meadowgrasses from the same rootstocks that had probably fueled horses still carpeted the floor beneath the trees. There were stone walls, of course: one that even ran down into the swamp, which therefore could not have been very old. At the end of the path was a great big hole. A ten-year-old girl I later showed it to suggested that it was made by a falling star, but I'm pretty sure it is a cellar hole for an outbuilding dating back to the time of the Finches.

Up on the ridge the soil was too thin to have ever been farmed. In places the rock cropped out, striated by the glaciers that had slid over them on their way south. On the north side of the ridge the rock had the dunelike smoothness characteristic of *roches moutonnées*, but on the south side it was cracked by the ice and some of it later weathered and broke off, rolling down to the level midslopes below. Several dozen ancient chestnut oaks stood on the ridge. Most of them were dead. The thick, dark cracked bark had peeled away from the stout, dead columns, to reveal black strands of mycelium creeping up the naked wood. Once I heard the hysterical laughter of a pileated woodpecker as he was ripping open one of the uppermost boughs in search of ants.

While the exact story of their death will never be learned, the trees had been on the ridge for more than a century, long enough to have taken most of the nutrients out of the soil. The five-year drought that came early in the nineteen-sixties must certainly have weakened them, but it was probably the gypsy-moth outbreak later in the decade that finished them off. These insects had been slowly spreading over New England since their dozen progenitors escaped in 1867 from the laboratory of a man in Massachusetts who had brought them over from France to see if he could make silk from their cocoons. You could go up to a ridge at the height of the outbreak and listen to the caterpillars chewing up chestnut oaks and hornbeams, to thousands of droppings—frass, as the stuff is called—spattering the dry leaves on the floor. It sounded like a hard rain, only the sky was perfectly clear.

At first the trees would keep putting out new leaves, two or three times in a season. But after several summers of repeated defoliation they just couldn't do it anymore. Various enemies moved into the region to take care of the millions of caterpillars. There were explosions in the populations of black and yellow-billed cuckoos, of the calasoma beetle, and of a certain wasp that preys on gypsy-moth larvae. But the caterpillars' greatest enemy was *Bacillus thuringiensis*, a bacterium which entered their stomach tracts and kept them from eating until they were found by the thousands all over the woods, dead of starvation, curled up and dangling from branches by threads. By the time the scourge had been checked, it was too late for the chestnut oaks at Brookside.

71

Under the massive dead trees now a hot, dry sproutland of saplings contends for their places—all manner of little beeches, birches, maples, and oaks. With such an abundance of growing tips on the ridge, it is not surprising that the deer have made a whole system of paths there along which they browse silently and invisibly. I often find their signs in the woods or in the garden—a hoofprint in the snow or soft ground, a sapling grown awry in an attempt to recover from the loss of its lead shoot, a patch of jewelweed neatly clipped to a height of two feet, or the lower buds missing from a rhododendron. Once I returned to find a doe standing in the driveway. As Westchester was released from cultivation, the deer multiplied. "The many deer seen in recent years between the Hudson and Connecticut valleys are not of the native stock of this region, but come from an unexplained migration from the north," James Wood wrote in 1917. "They will probably disappear as mysteriously as they have come."

Early in the morning five or six deer arise from their dormitory in a locust grove and venture into the fields of the old Cook Estate on the other side of the ridge to nibble timothy grass and wildflowers. The fields now belong to a man who proposes to turn them into a development of three hundred and fifty luxury condominiums. But the townspeople have been fighting him for the last few years, and his plans are tied up in the courts down in White Plains. Nobody knows what's going to happen.

One Saturday morning my wife and I were wandering through the second of the seven fields, when we met head-on with a fine six-point buck on the run. Behind him, yelping their heads off, were two frenzied beagles. We waited for the buck to bound past us and into the swamp, then jumped in front of the dogs, which stopped in their tracks and immediately lay on their backs, cringing. We picked up their tags, checked the address, and shooed them back home in the direction of Armonk.

I think I know what became of that buck. Two weeks after we had met it in the fields I gave a busload of schoolchildren a tour of the sanctuary. I showed them the evidence of the Wisconsin Glacier and the big old chestnut oaks dead on the ridge, and walked them over to the Finch cellar hole. Suddenly, one of the older boys, who had been holding hands with two girls in the rear, came running up with a patch of white fur he'd found on the path. Another girl let out a scream. There in the cellar hole, staring up at us from under a mound of leaves, was the clouded blue eye of a dead deer.

The game warden came by that afternoon and tried to piece together what had happened. After a long examination he finally broke the silence: "Been dead at least two weeks." I described the buck the beagles had been running a few weeks earlier, and he agreed that this might have been the same animal. "He could've kept running through the swamp, jumped the guard rail onto the road, and been hit." He turned over the carcass and showed me how the right shoulder had been crushed by some terrible blow. Somehow, though, the buck had managed to hobble back into the swamp and partway up to the cellar hole before it expired right on the path. Someone had found him there, sawed his antlers off, dragged the rest of him into the hole, and buried him over with leaves.

"What'll I do with him?" I asked.

"Leave him there. The animals will take care of it."

Every time I walked past the cellar hole after that, there would be a little less of the deer. First, the hindquarters were gone; then the rib cage had been gnawed clean and dragged across the hole. By the time the first snow fell, only the head was left, and there were dog tracks of various sizes all around. Some of them looked as if the big round paws of the neighbor's black Labrador had made them. In the spring I brought a friend who had an electronic metal detector to sound out the cellar hole for old coins, tools, and nails. We found none, but thirty yards back in the woods I saw the bleached skull of the deer lying on a lush carpet of clubmoss—the only physical evidence that the incident had ever happened.

6 Bitten by
a Copperhead

Every place has it dangers. In the Amazon it's the snakes, the jaguars, and the stinging insects. But Westchester is perhaps the most treacherous environment of all, a nice, safe womb where you can survive comfortably with a minimum of expended energy. Nothing is demanded of you. Nature usually keeps its place.

But one morning a young housewife in obvious distress drove up in a red compact ranch wagon and ran down the walk with a little girl in one hand and her pocketbook in the other. Between gulps for air she told me that her daughter had found a little snake on their doorstep and her husband had beheaded it with the edge of his shovel. She had it in a jar in the car and would I please come and take a look at it. "Okay," I said somewhat irritably, because I suspected that human fear and ignorance had caused the death of another harmless and probably even beneficial snake. The last snake someone had brought me was a baby hognose, a particularly docile and friendly species which the man of the house had also decapitated with a shovel. Whenever West-chesterites see a snake, which isn't very often, their immediate reaction is to assume that it's a copperhead and to beat it to death with the nearest thing they can lay their hands on. The chances of the poor snake's being a copperhead are very slim. It's more likely to be a milk snake, a water snake, or a hognose. In thirty years I've only run into one copperhead in the wild. I was telling the woman all this when she took the jar out of a paper bag and, my God, it was a copperhead. With its alternating bands of copper and a ruddier brown, bulging and getting thinner in an hourglass pattern, its flat, wedged-shaped head with a vertical black pupil set in a yellow iris, and the yellow tip of the tail which young copperheads have—there was no doubt about it. It looked venomous, and it was.

Copperhead bites are not normally fatal except to small children and people with bad hearts. The snakes are rare and retiring, striking only when cornered and persistently annoyed, so they're not much of a problem. But this one had been lying right on their doorstep. It must have been sunbathing, which the snakes do in the spring and again in the fall, remaining more nocturnal during the hot summer months.

I wanted to see where the snake had been found, so the woman got back into her car and I followed in mine. Her house was up on a ledge and had a nice view. An oak-hickory forest shared the hillside with patches of hemlock and beech. It was copperhead country, all right. They prefer ravines and rocky ledges.

"You probably have more," I told the woman, "but you may never see one again. This is the sort of place where they like to den. But they're very shy and mild-tempered and will keep out of your way if you give them a chance." I gave her the name of a friend who likes to catch poisonous snakes in his spare time and who might be willing to take any more that might be around off her hands.

The northern copperhead goes by the Latin name of *Agkistrodon mokeson mokeson*. There are three other subspecies of copperhead besides the northern one: the southern copperhead, *Agkistrodon contortrix contortrix*; the broad-banded copperhead, *Agkistrodon mokeson laticinctus*; and the Trans-Pecos copperhead, *Agkistrodon mokeson pictigaster*. There's also an osage copperhead in the southern lowlands, so called because it is bright orange. Several herpetologists are lobbying to get subspecific status for it, too. Taken as one species, these snakes cover a larger territory than any of the other fourteen poisonous species in the United States. If you were to draw a line from the northeastern tip of

76

Massachusetts to Pittsburgh, and from Pittsburgh to the extreme southeastern corner of Nebraska, you would get a rough idea of the northern boundary of their range. If you then drew a line from the extreme southeastern tip of Nebraska to the upper Rio Grande in Texas, passing just southeast of New Mexico, you would be tracing their western boundary. South and east of those two lines you stand a chance of running into them.

Being the most widely distributed venomous snake in the United States, the copperhead also accounts for the most bites. About sixty-five hundred people a year are treated for copperhead bite. Of these only fifteen—one-fourth of one percent—die. In 1967 nineteen people were bitten by copperheads in the state of New York. That would be 1.1 persons for every million of population. None of the bites resulted in death. The state which reports the greatest number of bites every year is North Carolina.

The potency of venomous snakebites is measured in terms of the minimum lethal dose (MLD) that will kill a rat. Copperheads have a high MLD of 10.50 milligrams. The eastern diamondback rattlesnake, which is responsible for most of the fatalities in the United States, has an MLD of 1.89 milligrams, while the coral snake, our country's most deadly reptile, has an MLD of only 0.99. The venom is modified saliva which helps the snake procure and digest food; its defensive function is secondary. It is made up of complex proteins and enzymes that defy full chemical analysis, and like the venom of most pit-vipers (the copperhead is a rattleless pit-viper) it is primarily hemotoxic, working through the bloodstream, and not neurotoxic, like the coral snake's. The venom is manufactured by a gland behind the eye. By contracting the muscles around the gland the snake sends the fluid down through a duct and out into the fangs, which are long, hollow, and as sharp and efficacious as hypodermic needles. The fangs are attached to a movable bone at the front of the upper jaw. When not in use they are folded like hinges against the roof of the mouth, but they can be erected quickly for striking. A row of smaller teeth extends along the jawbone behind the front fangs. If a fang is broken off, pulled out, or shed (which happens every six weeks or so; the fangs are often found in the snake's feces) it takes only a few days for a replacement to move into place.

If it has time, the copperhead will coil into striking position, throwing up its head and some of its length in an S-shaped loop and rattling its tail as do many nonpoisonous snakes; it behaves somewhat like a dog snarling and raising the hair on its spine when threatened. Like the boxer's stand, this position enables it to strike with maximum speed, force, and reach—about a third of its length. Take heed, however: The snake does not have to be in a coil to bite. It can even envenomate you by reflex action after it is dead. Once they have made contact, the jaws close down, injecting the amount of venom the snake feels it needs.

Doctors diagnose the bite's severity by the "two p's"—puncture wound and pain—and the "two e's"—edema and erythema, which mean swelling and reddening. There may be one, two, three, four, or more fang punctures, depending on the nature of the bites and the number of times you've been bitten. Edema usually develops within the first thirty minutes. Hemorrhagic blebs may arise around the bite. The victim may suffer nausea, vomiting, shock, diarrhea, numbness, and tingling around the mouth, muscle fasciculations around the bite, coma, abnormal bleeding, and renal failure. There are four degrees of venenation. Grade 0 is no venenation. Grade 1 is minimal venenation with one to five inches of e and e around the bite. Grade 2 is moderate with six to twelve inches of e and e. Grade 3 is severe with more than twelve inches of e and e.

Often the snake will inflict a dry bite without any venom at all; whether because its glands are empty or out of the kindness of its heart there is no way of knowing. After it has bitten the snake waits for its victim to die. The poison doesn't take long to act on a small animal. If it's a mouse the snake will let go and back off, because mice can bite back. If it's a bird, the snake holds on, because birds can fly away. Copperheads also eat frogs (but not toads, which are toxic), salamanders, shrews, moles, an occasional chipmunk or squirrel, and a variety of insects, including cicadas, spiders, moths, and caterpillars, which do not require the use of venom. During the year of the locust they've been known to gorge themselves.

They're a funny snake. In spite of the fact that they're venomous they persist in residential areas. In Westchester County they're found as far down-country as north White Plains. In fact the world record *Agkistrodon mokeson mokeson* was taken in White Plains in the thirties. It was fifty-three inches, twenty-three inches longer than the average adult. The second longest *mokeson* on record was collected in the Mianus River Gorge, in Bedford, New York, a few years ago by Mike Tkacz, the county's foremost expert on poisonous snakes. It was forty-four inches. It died recently, and Tkacz has it pickled in his refrigerator.

Copperheads are the only venomous species in my county. There used to be timber rattlers, but Bill Sitka, a maintenance man at the Pound Ridge Reservation, killed what was probably the last one in 1958. The copperhead persists in our populous area because it's on a completely different wavelength from human beings. From mid-October to the end of April it hibernates. A den can be anywhere from six to a couple of hundred snakes and it is usually in a cave or crevice in a rock outcrop or some rugged, wooded area. Sometimes copperheads will den together with pilot black snakes, which is how the superstition that "pilot" blacks will lead you to a copperhead den got started. This may be true, but only sometimes. Another belief, that copperheads smell like cucumbers, is without foundation.

Upon emergence from hibernation at the beginning of May, the copperheads' first priority is mating. Ledges become the scene of combat dances. Two males will stand up, like cobras, as high as they can and push against each other, trying to knock the other over. No biting takes place and neither snake is hurt. It's only a show of strength. The loser of the combat dance doesn't lose his chance to copulate, however, as the combatants aren't fighting over a particular female and there are dozens of partners waiting in the den. Directly beneath the anal plate, in the first subcordials, each male has hemipenes, a divided penis, so that upon entwining with a female he can enter her from either side. Copulation is a long, involved process. The two snakes can be entwined for several days.

For the rest of May both sexes do little except bask on sunny ledges. By June the danger of frost is over—a snake caught out in a frost could easily lose its life—and the males disperse, traveling as far as a mile from their den, which is quite a distance for a snake. During the early summer they visit every habitat, looking for mice. They like to sit in a crevice, coiled and half-hidden by leaves, where they can intercept their mainstays, short-tailed shrews and white-tailed mice as they scurry under the leaves. Much of their hunting is done at night, when their thermo-receptive facial pits take over, leading them to mammalian prey.

These pits are, of course, worthless against a frog or other cold-blooded creatures. Overnight campers in the woods have rolled over on copperheads that were attracted to the warmth of their bodies, and been bitten. Copperheads feed about once a week. They have extremely low metabolisms and don't move much except when they have to procure a mouse or something. A healthy snake could probably go for a year without eating.

While the males are roaming the gravid females don't generally stray very far from the den. Late in August or early in September they deliver three to nine young. Each infant is born in his own membranous fetal sac and they are extruded one at a time, about every eight minutes. They average nine inches, the last inch or so being bright yellow. Herpetologists are not in agreement about the reason for the yellow tail, but it may serve to attract wood frogs, on which juvenile copperheads feed almost exclusively. The yellow tail disappears after the second or third shedding, at about the same time that the young snakes begin to develop an appetite for other creatures of the forest floor. Adult copperheads usually shed their skin twice a season, juveniles more often because they are growing faster. The venom of a juvenile is faster-acting and probably more toxic, but delivered in less quantity, so the bite of a little snake will have roughly the same effect as that of a big one.

I know of only three people who were bitten by a copperhead in Westchester County: Bart Bouricius, Richie Hawthorne, and his older brother John. John was bitten deep in the woods. He was alone at the time and he came close to dying. Bart and Richie were bitten on Wednesday, August 14, 1963. They were both fourteen and deeply interested in snakes. Across from Richie's house in Cross River was a field that had just been cut and the two boys were searching in a haystack for mice to feed their pet pilot black snake when they uncovered the first copperhead. Bart was so used to catching snakes that, by conditioned reflex, he shot out his hand and grabbed it. "I only thought once," he recalled, "If I'd thought twice I probably wouldn't have done it." Nevertheless Bart had the snake behind the head before it could strike. At that moment Richie turned up another copperhead and Bart, with the first snake wriggling in one hand, shot out a foot and tried to pin the other one down, but he didn't step close enough to the head. It turned around and bit him just above the rim of his sneaker. Not realizing that Bart had been bitten, Richie grabbed for the snake and was bitten on the third finger of his right hand. All this happened in about three seconds.

"We carried the snakes across the road to Richie's house and dropped them into a garbage can and put the lid on it," Bart went on. Then they made straight-line incisions and proceeded to suck. Bart put his foot into his mouth and sucked, while Richie sucked his finger. Richie's brother went off on his motorcycle and got the doctor. The doctor took them to the nearby Ward Pound Ridge Reservation where they were given antivenin. But there were only five ampoules, enough for only one person. Luckily Dr. Dowling, the curator of reptiles at the Bronx Zoo, lived nearby and was able to bring some more antivenin on his way home.

The bites didn't begin to hurt till about two hours later. Up till then the boys had simply been excited and rather proud. But gradually Bart's leg swelled up to the knee like a balloon and turned black, blue, and yellow, and Richie's hand grew and turned color. Richie's bite, however, was not as serious as Bart's, probably because he had been the snake's second victim. They spent four days in the hospital, then they got better.

The copperhead that bit them was a thirty-seven-inch-long female. She turned out to be gravid, producing eight babies a few days after being placed in the garbage can. The snake and its litter were presented to the American Museum of Natural History, where they were stuffed, mounted, and placed in a diorama. They are on exhibit to this day.

Although there is considerable controversy about the best way to treat a copperhead bite, the way Bart and Richie went about it was pretty much correct. The first thing you do is lie still. Any movement speeds up the spread of the venom through the bloodstream. Within three minutes you should make a straight incision, one-eighth of an inch deep and one-quarter of an inch long, in each fang mark to open up the wound, and start sucking. The longer and harder you suck, the better. If, however, you have any cuts or cold sores in your mouth, you could envenomate yourself. Venom can enter the bloodstream especially easily through the capillaries of the lips. Venom swallowed into the digestive tract, however, is harmless. Some people say you should also tie a tourniquet between the bite and the heart, loosening it every ten minutes and never having it so tight that you can't put a finger through it. With a tourniquet tighter than that you risk gangrene.

Packing the bite with ice—cryotherapy—retards the spread of the venom but kills more tissue, so its desirability is debatable. Neutralizing the venom by injecting polyvalent crotaline antivenin into the bloodstream is unquestionably helpful. Antivenin is usually serum from a horse which has been immunized against rattlesnake poison. But if you are allergic to antivenin, *it* can kill you, so it is a good idea to have a skin test first. Antibiotics and tetanus shots are also advisable, since the mouth of the snake may harbor pathogens.

In the final analysis, mechanical removal—the good old "cut and suck" method—is probably the most important part of the treatment. It has been shown that enough venom can be removed from a bite by incision and suction to kill a second experimental subject, which should convince anybody.

7 A Year on the Land

One of the good things about living in Westchester, or anywhere in the Northeast, for that matter, is the unfolding of the seasons. You don't have to work at it to feel grounded in a particular time of year; you don't have to stop and think what month you're in. Each season has its own persuasive momentum; before you know it, spring is here, and you can't even remember what it was like when the trees were bare and frost had buckled the turf. It's a full-time job keeping up with the daily changes.

January 11. The warmest on record—sixty-three degrees at 7:30 p.m., four degrees warmer than the previous high set in 1933. I went out to the second field of the old Cook estate and stood on the rise, several feet from the spot where a lone, terribly rare blunt-leaved milkweed had sprouted up the summer before, causing a small sensation among area wildflower lovers. Suddenly an intense bright object appeared in the east, started to move across the lower sky as if in slow motion, leaving a long trail, and after a period of time in which I could have counted to five, had my breath not been held in, disappeared. It was too bright and close to be a comet, too far and fast to be a plane.

January 12. I called up my friend Tim Ferris, who is writing a book about the sky, and he said it must have been a "fireball," no bigger than your fist, coming in at a flat angle and burning itself out in the atmosphere. They are also called "bolide meteors" or just "bolides" for short. That same night one of my most enthusiastic students was attacked by a male barn owl while playing a recording of a barn owl's call in a white pine plantation. The owl came down, thinking it was an interloper of its own species. Owls, like kingbirds, are interspecific territorial defenders. They'll attack anything—dogs, humans, milk trains, or at least hoot back at them. Lin went to school proudly showing everyone his shredded coat sleeve.

January 20. I think I saw a red-bellied woodpecker. The size and shape were right. I know they're in here. They've nested here in Leonard Park for the last two years. I first saw one right above the amphitheater, while conducting a public birdwalk. It was larger than a hairy and smaller than a flicker. The red mane and ladder-back, were unmistakable. Nobody believed me. But that afternoon a neighbor called to say that she had a red-bellied at her feeder. I hotfooted it over to her house and there it was, pecking at the suet. Later I learned to listen for the birds' juicy cluck in the woods, and tracked them to their nesting hole in a big barkless oak in a swale in Leonard Park. Next year they chose another tree in the same swale to nest in. From July through March they disperse.

Every year several more of these birds are reported in Westchester. At this moment they're one of our rarest permanent residents. The pair at Leonard Park is one of about a dozen reported to be nesting in the county. Red-bellieds are the latest in a long line of southern species which have been expanding their ranges. The cardinal started to do it in the forties and fifties. The tufted titmouse followed suit in the sixties. So did the turkey vulture. Most recently the mockingbird and the Carolina wren have moved up in quantity, and they're no longer unusual. White-eyed vireos, blue-gray gnatcatchers, hooded warblers, and Louisiana waterthrushes are doing it too but they're only here in the summer and not in significant numbers. There are several possible explanations for the presence of these southern birds here: the mitigated winters, the return of the Central Hardwood Forest, human encroachment on their habitat, bird-population pressures in their range, the sudden boom in suburban bird feeders. Mockingbirds, which have no trouble relating to man, have benefited from the growth of suburbia and from the increased planting of holly trees, of ornamental crab apples, and of multiflora roses along highway baffles. The cuckoo, uncommon under ordinary circumstances in the area, is enticed north in larger number by periodic outbreaks of the tent caterpillar. No one knows yet why red-bellied woodpeckers have suddenly found Westchester to their liking. Perhaps they are filling the niche of the red-*headed* woodpecker whose numbers here have shrunk to practically nothing due to competition from starlings for their nesting holes.

January 26. The sky stays blue at sunset on a cold winter day. The frost on the wood sparkled like cut grass as we walked out into the marsh on the creaky boardwalk.

During the winter months the interior of one's house becomes more important, the placement of objects, the way the light comes in through the window. I take a motherly interest in the animals that decide to spend the winter in our house. The flying squirrels in the attic, the small black lady beetle, *Olla abdominalis plagiata*, which likes to explore my little red table. There's a bunch of spiders that spin black thatches in the corners of the rooms.

Our bird feeder is right at the study window. That's the price they have to pay. People think it's really important to feed the birds, but I wonder. After all, the birds have been getting along for millions of years without our assistance. The big thing, everybody says, is that once you've started feeding them, don't stop, or you'll starve them to death. I wonder about that, too. If I quit putting seed in my tray, they'd probably just fly over to my neighbor's. Let's face it: The reason we feed the birds is that we like to have them around.

February 12. Fifteen percent of the kids are home with the flu, *A. victoria*, a particularly virulent strain. The rest of us have been marooned at the school in a sudden blizzard. February is a good month to be away. A few minutes ago a snowy owl, with a crow in hot pursuit, flew over the library. A rare winter visitor, the snowy sometimes drifts down, mostly along coastal marshes, as far south as the Carolinas. This year they were sighted on Jones Beach, Long Island. This snowy had probably been driven back north by

85

the storm, which came up from the South. Other strays were caught in the blizzard: hermit thrushes, grackles, and a Carolina wren, whose tail was drooping wretchedly. The southern wrens are decimated in snowstorms.

February 13. Ginny Weinland, a superb wildflower photographer from Chappaqua, and I walked to Hidden Valley in Ossining, one of Westchester's premier wild spots. Like the Mianus Gorge in Bedford and the Halle Ravine in Pound Ridge, it's steep-walled, a hemlock-beech forest with an ericaceous layer. Ginny is telling me about the Fibonacci number series in nature which occurs in a 1-1-2-3-5-8-13 sequence (the next number is the sum of the two previous ones) and determines the helixes and spirals of shells, the articulation of leaves on branch, the seed arrangements of pine cones and sunflowers, and many other structures. I tell her about my great-uncle, Andre Avinoff, a lepidopterist and watercolorist from whom I inherited a love of nature, who was working on a book on the significance of pattern in living forms when he died. He had a hypometric theory about it.

Ginny discovers a delicate highbush blueberry in an open spot among the laurels. The twigs grow out at right angles and all in the same plane, and are tipped with big and little buds. The former will be flowers, the latter leaves. The branches show the multilayering typical of plants growing in the open. Ginny takes a picture of this very Oriental-looking shrub against the snow. In the swamp we find canine prints running in a straight line—fox. The rim of an ice-shelf reflected in the still water becomes another subject for her Nikkormat. Here it's cool and wet enough for yellow birches and there is one old giant leaning over the swamp at a crazy angle, hollow at the base. Hard to understand what keeps it up. Yellow birches have more repoussé lenticels than black birches, and the bark peels off in flaky sheets. There are some colossal tulip trees here whose golden flower goblets catch the sun. Their bark is bleached out in some patches, in others coated with lavender algae. The older ashes have the same hypopigmentation, and the mascles on their bark are edged with lavender.

February 21. The geese are moving. I saw three skeins with over fifty birds in each over a swamp below Armonk, headed toward the eastern sun soon after dawn.

February 26. The redwings are back. The dull browns and ochers of dead grass on the fairways of the Maple Moor golf course in Mamaroneck give way to the soft green sheen of new growth. Plant life turns green along roadsides first due to retention and reflection of heat by pavement. Along the Hutchinson River Parkway the Canada geese peck at the stubble, with their necks curved delicately like the handles of a vase.

March 7. Today is the first inkling of spring. With patches of snow still on the ground the first butterfly, a mourning cloak, had come out of hibernation. Tonight the spotted salamanders will probably creep down to the vernal pools and lay their egg masses, the size of a golf ball or bigger, attaching them to twigs in the water. They look like miniature black dinosaurs with yellow spots and spend their whole life underground except for two nights in February or March after the first warm rain. About the time the wood frogs start up their flat double quack, they come out and lay their eggs.

Halfway up a ridge I found the winter catkins of the hazelnut expanded into longer male blossoms. On top of the ridge it was drier and they were still catkins. A week later, crimson strands will have sprouted from other buds on the hazelnuts. These will be the female flowers.

March 13. The peepers are quaking in the wet spots. It's deafening—a real cacophony. The pussy willows are opening.

March 18. Spring begins in the marsh, in water, the medium of birth. Swamp maples are the first to turn red (flowers) in the spring and the first to turn red (leaves) in the fall. Silver, swamp, Norway, and sugar maples bloom in that order, but their inconspicuous wind-pollinated flowers are ignored by the general public.

March 23. Palm Sunday. Last time at this year in the sunlit portions of the swamp, the skunk cabbage leaves had not yet come out. This year they have already reached a height of ten inches. Springtails or snow fleas are mobbing the water-filled tractor ruts in the second field of the old Cook estate. Crocus, snowdrops, and scilla are out in the garden. So are primula and andromeda. The house finches, sometimes called western linnets (they were intro-

87

duced from California) are in full twitter. Along the brook the green cones of helibore buds stick up in the moss like nipples surrounded with brown bristles. A woodpecker's rattling tattoo drifts in the wind. The male hazelnut flowers have shot their spores. At my approach the peepers stop. Do they detect intruders by sound or sight? The chickadee's call is urgent, frequent, penetrating.

April 10. The trout is back under the bridge. Cold, windy, clear for the last week. The trees are still bare, the wood empty except for fat, wind-blown robins, crows, sparrow, jays. The aspen are in flower.

April 20. Honeysuckle is the first to put out leaves. Spicebush is about out. The white-toward-purple petals of the round-leaved hepatica have blossomed in their oaky soil, the delicate influorescences of the dwarf ginseng have opened to the shafting sunlight. Trilliums have leafed out in sheltered nooks, their flowers giving off the smell of carrion which appeals to their pollinators. Bloodroot, coltsfoot, spring beauty, trout lily, bluet, sweet white violet, pachysandra, marsh marigold, daffodil, dandelion—all are in flower. It is astonishing, the difference that one week makes. The blue-brown "turkey-tail" polypore is in fruit. The glossy dark green leaves of the wild leek are up, and the new leaves of the crinkleroot which have a waxy sheen, like black mud the morning after rain before it begins to dry and crack. The Dutchman's-breeches and the shadbush—"a tall candle burning in a shadowy room"—come out on this day of drenching sun, a Sunday.

April 25. Returning through the woods we come upon an old coon who could hardly move. He was in the last stages of distemper. Tame and wobbly, he was standing near a stone wall, right next to a green, algae-smeared bottle from the Oriental Bottling Co., Harrison, New York. I went up and stroked his back with a branch. No response. His eyes were cloudy green (cataracts?) and it was doubtful if they could see. I passed the stick in front of them and his face would only move back and forth slightly. Above us, flickers were mating, chuckling in the upper branches. A Cooper's hawk flew up and then was whisked downwind by a gust. Not knowing what else to do we left the coon there to die.

The next day I returned to find the coon lying on his side,

breathing stertorously. So, thinking I was doing the animal a favor, I "put him out of his misery," coshing him many times on the head with a rock till he no longer moved. He didn't even have enough life in him to defend himself. Perhaps it was wrong to interfere with the slow, quiet ending. A few days later a woman called about a "young coon whimpering in the bushes." Westchester is overpopulated with coons, which are equally at home in the town, the backyard, and the forest. They give each other distemper very easily, and the dogs that tangle with them as well.

They say ninety-five percent of the animal kingdom comes out at night. This is especially true of environments like suburbia where people are in the habit of destroying snakes, deer, and other wildlife. At night a whole new shift takes over. The barred owl assumes the niche of the red-shouldered hawk, watching from the same branch for movements or rodents on the floor below. I've often heard the tarryhooting and caterwauling of a barred owl in the swamp, but never seen one. Last night at eight my naturalist friend Julio de le Torre conducted an "owl prowl." He promised to show at least a screech owl to the thirty men, women, and kids who followed him down the path along the swamp and out to the field flashing their torchbeams every which way as if it were London at wartime and searching the sky for bombers.

He stopped us at the edge of a field with a finger to his lips and whispered, "Everybody turn off your lights and be still." He gave me a stick with a stuffed red-phase screech perched on it and told me to hold it up. Holding it against the sky in the moonlight I felt like a high priest in some animistic ceremony. He flicked on his tape recorder, playing the eerie wail of a screech owl, rewinding it and playing it again over and over for some five minutes. Then he shut it off and listened. Then he began ululating the love calls himself. It was very convincing. Along with his other accomplishments he is an opera singer.

The screeches were completely beguiled. One called back from the other side of the ridge, another from the swamp. Their answers seemed to be coming from very far away, but screech-owl calls are deceptive. The birds call loud from afar and softer when up close. He said he was sitting in his car late one night and listening to a wail which he thought was at least three hundred yards away, when he turned to find the owl right in front of him looking at him from a distance of no more than the length of his arm. Screeches are very friendly and very curious. I've had one follow me through the woods, hopping along from branch to branch.

Suddenly, "There he is," he whispered excitedly, and flicking on his torch, directed it to where the bird stood on a hickory branch. He stayed there long enough for everyone to get a good look at him, then angled off into the darkness. "They're probably mates," he said. "Sometimes the mated pairs will harmonize, with the female lower-pitched by a third or a fifth." Julio and his wife can do the duet together. Several times as we walked on we heard flying squirrels, the screech owl's most frequent victim, chattering from their tree cavities. It was a warm, dry night and the leaves were crackling all around us.

May 1. The psychological effect of flowers bursting into color and the birds bursting into song is overpowering. Vividly yellow orioles sing in midair and from treetops. The veeries, the most audible thrushes in Westchester, have begun their clear, liquid, descending song, attenuated like sections of a telescope. The cardinals are singing their jumbled scalloped notes. The titmice are whistling away. Self-conscious exhibitionists, the catbirds sound, when they first come up, like the parrots with whom they've been wintering in the tropical jungle. After a few weeks they will begin to mimic the woodthrushes and the towhees. The two other mimic thrushes—brown thrashers and mockingbirds— are also active. The catbird sings his phrase once, the thrasher twice, and the mockingbird will repeat it up to five times. Kids are surprised to learn that chickadees spend four-fifths of their lives upside down and eat up to a hundred thousand spider eggs a day apiece. Chickadees, phoebes, and titmice, I tell them, are the easiest birds to exchange calls with in the forest.

May 6. It is dogwood time in the north-county. It has already been dogwood time in the south-county for several days. The flowers are either snow-white or creamy green. The forest has leafed out. Mycologists comb the margins for the most prized of all edible mushrooms—*Morchella esculenta* and *Morchella angusticeps* —craterous purple-brown cones on phallic shafts. The most delicious of all mushrooms, the morels, come up when the May apples bloom (others say when the oak leaves are feathering), but this is not always reliable. By the end of May many more flowers and mushrooms have cropped up, a certain species at a certain time, to remind you of the plan. There are maiden pink, stargrass, and other events in the field.

May 29–31. Memorial Day. With the danger of frost over I put in my peppers and tomatoes. For a number of months I have been hearing noises in the wall each night, the sounds of wood being gnawed, of little feet scampering madly, of young animals screaming frailly and incessantly. Flying squirrels, I thought, and after checking the wiring and finding that it is wrapped in metal I gave it no more thought. Then a few weeks ago a large gray form dashed between the stove and the refrigerator. It was unmistakably a rat.

Now that I knew what was making them, the noises in the wall would set me on edge whenever I heard them, but still I took no steps. Encountering no resistance, the rats became bolder. They chewed a hole in the dining-room wall and in the morning I began to find the stand of spices and condiments in the kitchen scattered around and knocked over. Finally I began to see them, or think I saw them, regularly during the day. When I found one drinking out of the faucet in the bathroom sink I decided the rats had gone far enough.

Poison is not a good idea: The rat retreats to its hole and dies there, and you can never get rid of the smell. Better to get a few of the old whango-type traps. The boys at Kisco Paint and Hardware sold me one Victor Four-Way rat trap made by the Woodstream Corporation of Lititz, Pennsylvania, and two Can't Miss Four-Way mouse traps made by the McGill Metal Products Co. of Marengo, Illinois, and wished me luck.

The very first night I set the Victor on the kitchen counter I heard a loud snap about two in the morning, put on my bathrobe, and went down to investigate. Pinned under the wire and lifeless lay the biggest rat I'd ever seen. Somehow I had gotten the impression, maybe from the cartoons I had seen as a kid, that the varmint got caught by his tail. But no, it was the other way around. The cable had come down on the back of his neck. Death was probably instantaneous.

It must have been the head rat, because the next night all the other ones went on a rampage, and the next morning the house

91

was in shambles. The hook rug in the living room had been torn up, a dried cattail in a vase chewed to bits and the fluff had flown all over, two green candles had been knocked out of their holder and bitten in half, the edges of the cutting board in the kitchen had been gnawed, a leaf high up in the potted shefflera neatly snipped off. Pellets and rat urine all over the floor. The traps unsprung, but minus their bait. As I walked into the kitchen, one of them dashed out, bit my shoe on the sole, and ran back behind the frigidaire. It actually attacked me. It looked like I had a major insurrection on my hands. What should I do? Borrow a cat? Or a rat snake from my brother's museum? That wouldn't work. They only eat mice.

It turned out to be something quite different from a revolution. Later that day I found two young rats docile and defenseless in the wastebasket, exhausted from the struggle to get out. Another dead in a paper bag for no apparent reason. That day the traps knocked off three more, one of which was caught by the stomach, struggling pitiably. It was as if they were all giving themselves up in a final suicidal rush, like lemmings. I hear no gnawing or whimpering in the wall now, and the traps are set but unvisited. They were black rats, with gray fur and fierce black eyes and tails bigger than the rest of them, cleanlier and less aggressive than the Norway rats, the plague vectors whose tails are *shorter* than their bodies. Blacks nest in your attic, while the Norways prefer the cellar.

June 18. This evening I was going out to water the garden when I heard something in the redbud tree. There, among rustling, heart-shaped leaves, stood a small, intensely blue bird. The quick *tsick* coming from its throat and the nervous twitch of its tail seemed to be telling me to keep away. Another bird in the spruces began to answer, and when it jumped out to the tip of a branch I could see that it was drab brown and about as big as the first one. Indigo buntings. Bunting is a Victorian word. As in flags and bunting. Some gay fluttering material. Indigo is a rich blue, deeper than cerulean. I had always loved the resonance of these words, but had never seen the creature they described. As their name went through my mind, they flew into the woods, and I didn't see them again for several days. But all that summer I could hear the male's elaborate rhythmic utterances, starting at four-thirty in the morning and kept up till dusk, while his mate stayed out of sight. Whenever I walked into the garden the male would fly up into the dead, pitchforklike twigs of a high ash branch, keeping up an almost constant chatter. Maintaining this "hiccup stance" seemed to be his main duty. It served to keep the female posted of his whereabouts, to warn her of interlopers, and to intimidate the intruder himself. It also had sexual overtones. His song was varied, usually lasting from two to three seconds, with a ten-second interval. It resembled the yellow warbler's. Indigo buntings are strongly territorial, and song is the main mechanism for securing and defending a big enough breeding area. While the male stood his ground and hiccuped and sang, the female prepared a nest in the cinnamon ferns, and within a few weeks she could be seen bringing food to it. Early in the morning, they both liked to flutter around in the flower beds. By the end of July the male no longer woke me up and I saw no more of them.

July 11. A sudden violent hailstorm began at four-thirty and lasted no more than a few minutes, followed by torrents of rain for the next half hour. Pellets as big as small marbles snapped off many of the tomato vines, knocked the leaves out of the trees, and scattered them over the lawn.

There is heavy blooming in the fields. Wildflowers litter the meadows like handfuls of confetti. The woods had their turn. Now it is time for farb and grass to come forth. For the rest of the summer great sprays of color, vertiginous *dédoublements*, will sweep across the open places, culminating in the purple and yellow showers of aster and goldenrod. People like Dick Coe will be sitting in the middle of them on a bucket in front of an easel. A small, slow-spoken Southerner with a red nose and a pork-pie hat, Coe has quietly devoted his life to getting "the idea of them," and is now Westchester's foremost wildflower watercolorist. He paints with both passion and strict botanical fidelity, mixing the colors on the edge of an old porcelain plate at his side and applying them with a lot of water.

In the brightest fields the competition for pollinators is most intense. It's all really for the bugs. And because all fields in Westchester except for a few natural meadows are disturbed sites, half of the flowers are alien, the European and Asiatic cosmopolites that have followed men in their migrations—the Queen

93

Anne's laces, purple loosestrifes, and butter-and-eggs of this world. Their colors, smells, and other strategies multiply the bees' choices.

The most diverse fields are mowed only once or twice—often enough to keep the woody plants down and seldom enough to let whatever seeds are in them to make it into flowers. But land worth developing doesn't stay clear around here for long. The taxes are too high. The only open fields left either belong to very rich people or are tied up in legal complications, like the seven fields behind me. Here's a partial catalogue of what's out in the second field today: New Jersey tea, enchanter's nightshade, feverfew, cow vetch, hop clover, chickweed, racemed milkwort, black raspberry, rose campion (mullein pink), spotted Saint-John's-wort, onion grass, whorled loosestrife, fringed loosestrife, one blunt-leaved milkweed with curled, clasping leaves (a bee had gotten its legs stuck in the crevices between the tight flower petals and died there), butterfly weed, pale-spike lobelia, bog orchid (a small orchid, easily overlooked, with inconspicuous green flowers), Canada lily, wood lily (an arresting trumpet whose narrow, blood-red, black-flecked petals face up), the berries of the Tartarian honeysuckle, spreading dogbane. I have been following with fascination the growth of several poisonous water hemlock plants on the southern fringe. They are almost four feet now. The wet new leaves grow out from the purple-streaked stalks in fearfully symmetric groups of three.

This afternoon my father and I tried to count as many butterflies as we could. We were participating in a butterfly census of the entire Northeast. Neither the swallowtails nor the monarchs were out in force yet, but we found one monarch larva savaging a milkweed leaf, whose lactic juices make the butterfly impalatable to birds, enabling the tasty viceroy, in turn, to escape being eaten by mimicking it. Conclusions were hard to draw from the exercise: Because there is very little butterfly habitat in Westchester, their numbers are down from the mid-nineteen-fifties, but up from the sixties when the pernicious effects of DDT were having their greatest impact on the environment. But the return of fully forested conditions is offsetting to some degree the discontinuation of DDT. Nymphalids (fritillaries, ragged-edges, hunters, red admirals) and satyrids (wood nymphs and little wood satyrs) are just about the only butterflies in the county that will go into the woods.

We counted mostly in the second field and probably spotted no more than a fraction of the butterflies in it. There more than fifty of the following species: great spangled fritillary, aphrodite, little wood satyr, American copper, pearl crescent, northern cloudy wing, and silver-spotted skipper. Not having nets to catch them, we found the various species of *Polites* skippers and hairstreaks really hard to tell apart. But my father sifted through the field guide and picked out the minute marking that separate one species from the other. My father, who at one time considered entomology as a profession, has a rare subspecies of Jamaican hairstreak, found only in a few high sunny clearings of the rain forest, named after him—Shoumatoff's hairstreak. So he felt more confident about the hairstreaks than he did about the *Polites* skippers. Just after he had decided that two we were looking at were *gray* hairstreaks, a pair of men came riding up through the field—one on a bay, the other on a strawberry roan. "And what are we looking for today?" one of them said condescendingly. My father didn't even bother looking up. We counted two red admirals, one question mark, two species of geometrid moth, a couple of dozen cabbages, a few Pocahontas skippers, and a coral hairstreak. In a verge of tall bracken we came upon a swarm of banded hairstreaks, ten of them fluttering around in frenzied little balls, landing on the bracken and resting with their folded-up wings held not vertically, but in the peculiar manner of hairstreaks, to one side. "That was quite a find, wasn't it?" my father commented. "Ten hairstreaks all at once."

July 17. Today all the house wrens fledged in the thickets. I walked along the edges of the fields and found six broods of fluffy young clinging to branches, sometimes two or three ranged in a row on the same limb, not knowing what to do. I could have picked them off and held them in my hands, but I didn't.

July 18. A beautiful moth, *Haploa confusa*, on the doorsill. The lawn is at the height of its lushness and it needs cutting once a week now. I've had quite a struggle with that lawn. Martha Leonard's stonework below it changed its drainage dramatically. When I got here it was half dead, covered with a thick brown mat of old cuttings. Some would have called one of the dozen or so lawn doctors who roam around Westchester in vans with matching trailers in tow, rehabilitating people's ailing *gazons*. But I decided to do it myself. I rented a turfing machine that tore up the whole thing, thatch and all, leaving just the bare ground and a lot of wriggling worms. Then I raked it over and threw around some seed—a mixture of rye, fescue, and Kentucky blue. Next spring I had a whole new lawn.

Essentially a Victorian institution, the lawn was meant to provide a neat surface for such activities as picnicking, promenading, croquet, and tennis. But it also serves as a tame, formal layer of insulation against the full impact of wildness.

I don't really believe in lawns. You can become a slave to them. On Saturday afternoon in the summertime here, the contest between man and lawn is enacted in ten thousand yards across the county. The man out there in front of his house keeping his lawn in line and making his contribution to the overall respectability of the landscape is the quintessential image of suburbia. While many suburban men undoubtedly consider mowing their lawns to be a royal pain and would never get out there if their wives didn't constantly pressure them about it, I am fairly sure that an equal number secretly derive a deep satisfaction from reducing their territory to orderly rows of well-trimmed growth every week or so. There is considerable evidence that mowing the even rows is an important form of meditation and relaxation for the suburban man. You can unwind and let your thoughts take off behind the motor. Work up a good sweat.

August 1. The dog days of August are upon us. The month begins with a heat wave—high nineties, heavily humid, people passing out on the tennis courts. All the broad leaves of the deciduous forest are sweating massively through their pores. My head swims with the monotonous din of cicadas. Time perception is slowed way down. A set of tennis that takes only forty-five minutes by the clock seems to last eons.

There is renewed activity in the bird world. Families are about in the trees and thickets. Toward midmonth the songbirds go into hiding and molt clandestinely, staying under cover because they are vulnerable. The ticks are out in force this year. Every day I have to pull a few more bloated females off my dog's ears. So are the Japanese beetles. You find them in old fields devouring oak saplings and leaving only the brown skeletal veins of the leaves. The vegetation has peaked and the process of desiccation and withering and leaching out of chlorophyll is already underway.

Already late in July the mint family had begun to make their show. Now they continue with self-heal, mad-dog skullcap, giant blue hyssop, spearmint, peppermint, mountain mints like Virginia and narrow-leaved, and a dozen others which are hell to key out.

September 1. The summer has gone by so fast you wonder where it went to. The black swallowtails are barely able to flap their faded, tattered wings. You find them expiring in puddles.The shortening photoperiod is affecting the vegetation. Long-day plants like sweet clover and black-eyed Susan, needing more than twelve hours of sunlight to bloom, bloom no longer. But the shorter days have a pullulating effect on other flowers, particularly the asters, which have their finest hour during the first two weeks of the month, opening their lambent purple petals, their composite streamers, to the sun.

With less daylight the opportunity for photosynthesis is greatly diminished. The plants stop making chlorophyll. Photosynthesis breaks down and more stable pigments which are not proteins like anthocyanins (reds), carotenes (oranges), and xanthophyllums (yellows) become dominant in the leaf. Swamp foliage like that of red maples and black willows turns first because it is used to having more water.

September 20. At midnight four of us go to look for "foxfire." Foxfire is whatever glows in the night, especially certain phosphorescent slime molds. The second field is drenched in an unseasonably warm mist. The sky above is clear from a distance of twenty feet to infinity. We can barely make out the form of a big buck standing in the field some fifty yards away. Becoming aware of us he snorts into the mist and shoots off. We shine a light on the clover which, like most legumes, has lowered its leaves to the side of its stems for the night.

In the rich old woodland we see small lights pulsing in the darkness. Approaching one of them on hands and knees we discover that it is a glowworm. We crawl around over wet leaves and fallen timber, catch a few more, and take them back in a cigarette box for further examination. As we continue through the woods the box lights up in my shirt pocket whenever the juices ignite in the abdomens of the larval fireflies. We shine the light into the trees, moving it over the epiphytic mosses, lichens, and algae. To the side of the trail we see a faint but constant phosphorescence. It is a small gilled fungus growing on a decomposing stick of black birch. Real foxfire, as defined by *Webster's*: "the luminescence of decaying wood and plant remains, caused by various fungi."

October 1. It has been a good year for sprouted acorns and mushrooms. Almost every species of fungus known to the area cropped up. It rained at all the right times and the sun shined when it was supposed to; the sequencing of light and moisture needed for optimum hyphal growth was just right. Other kinds of sequencing are happening in October: Warm days will stimulate small populations of midges to hatch out here and there, even after frost has nipped the ferns. Quick breeders, these are probably the third or fourth generation of the year. There are hawks drifting through all month. First the buteos come in groups of from four to fifty, gliding from thermal to thermal, soaring in slow circles, with crows often escorting them through their territory. Then the accipiters, smaller and with longer, narrower tails, flapping more constantly. By mid-month there is "corn"— red berry clusters—on the jack-in-the-pulpit. The leaves stage a final, unforgettable show of color on the hillsides, the dogwoods turning maroon, the tulips bright yellow, the oaks and ashes an earthy brown. But it is the pumpkin domes of the sugar maples that make our northeastern autumn the most brilliant one in the world. And after the leaves have fallen, wispy, disheveled flower strands will sprout on the witch hazel.

October 10. A flash flood—four inches pour down on Friday afternoon. A motorist, swept from his car, drowns on the Hutchinson River Parkway. Downtown Mount Kisco is under three feet of water. People in the shoppers' parking lot can't open the doors to their cars. All the footbridges at Brookside are submerged, and I have to walk down the road to get to my house. By evening it subsides. This was a twenty-year storm which probably won't come around again for a good while. During the last big flood a little girl was sucked into a culvert near the Elks

Club as she was walking across a lawn to deliver the paper, emerging in the pond in front of the clubhouse two hundred yards later in shock but unhurt.

October 28. The leaves are ninety-five percent down. Lavender leaves are still clinging to the euonymus, and mauve translucent orange-pink leaves to the dogwood. The contours of the trees, suddenly revealed, come as something of a shock, and neighbors realize once again how close they live to one another.

November 17. The rhododendron leaves are curled like half-folded umbrellas. Three or four squirrels in a dogwood tree, pulling off berries. Later, a starling swarm descends and polishes off the whole tree in a few minutes. The only berries left now are the ones on the cranberry viburnum. They make good jelly, but are too tart for any animal. Walk into the woods now and you'll probably be joined by a little marauding band of chickadees. In these flocks there will be only one adult pair. The rest will be juveniles whose parents are elsewhere being foster parents to another brood. Just sit down and they'll find you within minutes. If you're willing to hold out the seed for twenty minutes without moving a muscle, they'll eventually muster up the courage to land on your hand. My brother's got such rapport with the chickadees at his museum that he can get them to take a sunflower seed from between his teeth. Here's how you do it: (1) Put the seed between your teeth; (2) brace a thumb against your chin and crook out your first finger to make a little landing platform for the bird; (3) make enticing noises with your lips, staying absolutely still otherwise.

December 25. A cold, boreal dawn over Snyder's Hill. The sky was green, the clouds pure rose, and by some optical illusion the sky seemed nearer than the clouds—like a lake or pool with clouds swimming in it. After lunch my brother and I go for a cross-country ski. The sudden snowstorm has been disconcerting for many birds. We come across a hermit thrush, a meadowlark, and a goshawk. In winter the light is not so strong but, as if to compensate, the trees have lost their leaves and the snow makes it much brighter. Today the light is almost blinding, and I can feel it on my face. Snow is the universal principle, the great equalizer, spreading over all the different communities and making them less distinguishable. I think of it as a gratuitous phenomenon and am grateful for its transformation, its temporary crystallization of the elements of the landscape. But the snow's not really as uniform as it seems. Its condition changes from one day to the next and is modified by the microclimate of each place. Around each tree a gully has been hollowed out by the Bernouilli effect— the way the wind, meeting an obstacle, rushes around it at a greater velocity, whisking snowflakes away like grains of sand from a stream bank. The snow is most uniform when frozen into a burnished crust, as it is today.

January 10. Westchester County is in the iceboating belt. The belt begins at Cape Cod, runs across southern Massachusetts and Connecticut, across the metropolitan area, through the Finger Lakes, across both shores of Lake Erie, and into lower Michigan (there's big action around Detroit) through Chicago, and winds up at Lake Mendota near Madison, Wisconsin. "You have to have thaws to knock the snow down to make the ice," Dick Andrews, commodore of the Westchester Ice Sailing Club, explained. "Otherwise it would be like having a skating rink that was never cleared off. It's got to be cold enough to freeze and warm enough to thaw." Three of four weekends a year, usually in January and February, it gets cold enough to have a regatta. There are seventy families in the Ice-Sailing Club. "We avoid the term 'boat' because we cover skate-sailers too."

Some lakes are ice-sailing lakes and some are ice-fishing lakes. Rarely do you find both activities on the same lake. In New Jersey some ice-fishermen put rings of sand around their holes so the sailors won't approach. The sand ruins their runners.

Cross River Reservoir is strictly an ice-fishing lake, and the fishing is by permit only. It's part of the New York water system, and skating is not allowed. But I have decided to risk it. The whole reservoir is frozen with an irresistible eight-inch film of black ice. If anyone catches me I'll just say I'm making a limnological study. It's ten below with the chill factor. Hard going, but completely safe. The ice varies from the color of milk to sheer transparent. The clear sections are scary. It feels as if there's no ice there at all. Ominous booms and groans travel the entire length of the reservoir, but that is only the ice shifting. It is really frozen. Only, way out in the middle there's a small circle of open water where several hundred waterfowl have gathered—gulls, black ducks, and a few buffleheads.

The bubbles trapped in the ice are methane and other gases of decomposition that are working their way toward the surface. Eventually they will be released, leaving the "honeycombs" typical of late winter ice. Then, as the land thaws, the reservoir will rise, and the ice film will crack and buckle into loose blocks and sheets.

With the wind behind me, I cover six miles in twenty-five minutes.

Part Two

The People

8 The Hub of Northern Westchester

There are six traffic lights in Mount Kisco, three supermarkets, roughly half a dozen ladies of the night, seven churches, two temples, and nine banks, none of which has ever been robbed. On summer evenings the local boys often get together at the diamond in the park for a game of slow-pitch softball. With their long hair in headbands and muscles bulging under their T-shirts, they play on teams sponsored by Flynn's Insurance, Mardino's Restaurant, and fourteen other local businesses. On winter afternoons the late sun lingers on the old corniced storefronts of West Main Street and catches the tiles on the spire of the Methodist Church, making them gleam like fish scales. With a busy business district and quiet, tree-lined back streets, it's a cozy little burg, small enough to know your neighbors, big enough to get lost downtown among strange faces.

Kisco means a "muddy place" in the Delaware Indian language, and most of Mount Kisco is bottomland on the floor of the Harlem valley. Until the seventeenth century it was the hunting ground of two Algonquian tribes and the inundated home of large numbers of beaver. Not much is known about these Indians except that—

unlike the Iroquois to the north—they didn't eat the flesh of their enemies and became warlike only when the Dutch began to destroy their villages. An early document suggests that Wampus, an Algonquian chief, lived in an elm-bark lodge about where the lodge of the Benevolent and Protective Order of Elks stands today. Arrowheads that residents of Mount Kisco have found in their backyards indicate that the area may have been a major campsite of an earlier tribe, between three and nine thousand years ago. By the eighteenth century the beaver were trapped out of the valley, and the Indians were massacred or scattered. Their descendants live on reservations in Oklahoma, Wisconsin, and Ontario. Only a handful can speak Delaware.

Around 1720 several families came up from Long Island and settled on the valley rim. One cluster of houses, called Kirbyville, sprang up about where the bowling alley is now. A second, Newcastle Corners, occupied the present site of Friendly's Ice Cream Parlor half a mile away. About the only outside contact the settlers had was with a missionary who would come up from the Episcopal Church of Rye every so often and preach to them. New Castle Corners grew faster because there a brook rushes steeply into the valley. By the nineteenth century the water was turning the wheels of a grist mill, a cotton mill, a woolen mill, and factories where needles, bricks, women's shoes, and men's shirts were manufactured. The largest concern at the Corners was the Spenser Optical Works. It is supposed to have been, at one time, the largest optical works in the country. It burned in 1877 and was then rebuilt, before finally leaving Newcastle in 1888. Children playing in the woods on Spenser Street occasionally unearth spectacles ground there a century ago.

In the 1840s the newly formed New York and Harlem Railroad Company decided to run a line of track up the Harlem valley. By 1847 there was rail service between 42nd Street, Manhattan, and New Castle Station, as it was called. With the New York City market only an hour and forty-seven minutes away, the dirt farmers in the surrounding country became dairy farmers, leaving their milk cans at New Castle Station early every morning. Little wood-frame houses spread block by block from the depot until soon the valley floor was covered with them. In 1848 Kirbyville, New Castle Corners, and the depot hamlet merged, taking the name Mount Kisco, after the bold, rocky bluff on the eastern rim of the valley. On the western bluff, Captain Merritt's Hill, there arose a number of impressive Victorian structures, on whose porches the well-to-do could sit of an August evening, listening to the katydids and gazing with satisfaction on the town that was burgeoning below them.

Westchester's period as an important center of dairy production did not last long. When the news broke out that the Erie Canal and the railroads had opened up the fertile reaches of the Midwest, it wasn't hard to persuade a farmer in the boulder-strewn Northeast to part with his spread and give up a life that had been difficult at best. By the 1880s the small, subsistence farmer was virtually extinct in Westchester.

But even as the farmers were leaving there was an influx of new people into the area. Much of the land was being bought up by New York businessmen who had done well enough to afford a place in the country. One country road outside of Mount Kisco, for example, was bought up by a Wall Street firm and parceled off among its senior partners. At the same time thousands of penniless immigrants from southern Italy were arriving at Ellis Island and making their way up into Westchester. Mount Kisco offered them plenty of opportunity. Laborers were being hired to build the Croton Dam, to man the factories and stack the wet walls that line the roads around Mount Kisco; some of the most beautiful stonework in the world is to be found in north-central Westchester. The Italians carted materials to the hilltops where splendid mansions were being erected. Some stayed on as gardeners after the estates were finished. Around the turn of the century a man named Petrillo was the main *padroni* or *agenti* for the immigrants. He would arrange for their passage, hire them out, and keep them in his boarding house for twelve dollars a week. Since they only made fourteen, and the balance was usually drunk at his bar, his protégés had few prospects. Then someone finally set off a keg of dynamite on Petrillo's porch and put an end to his exploitative operation.

Many of the Italians lived in a bustling ghetto called Sutton's Row (the site was recently smothered by a new Shopper's Bazaar and its enormous parking lot). From there it was a mile's walk to the Spenser Optical Works and the other factories in New Castle Corners where many of them worked. A few old-timers still remember the sound of the hobnails of the Italians' boots as they tramped through the village at dawn. Working conditions at the Corners were less than optimal, and during the 1880s the Italians staged several riots there. Then the work disappeared.

By 1888 Kirby Pond, the lake behind the dam, was stagnant and eutrophic, and the stench was becoming unbearable. Some people feared that it might become a breeding ground for malaria mosquitoes. Others were concerned about the "character hitherto unknown to the region" which the Italian "imports" were bringing to Mount Kisco. So Judge William Leonard, who owned the mill pond, had it thoroughly drained on December 4. Quinine sales dropped, but, even after the collapse of the industries at Newcastle Corners, the Italians kept coming.

In those days the cultural center of Mount Kisco was a general store by the name of Cox and Fish. The local sages would gather there around a big potbelly stove; armchairs and cuspidors were provided by the management. Next door was William Carpenter's Stationery Store. It flourished for four decades, but when Herman Fox and Morris Oxman took it over in 1928, it had fallen on bad times. Fox had immigrated from Argentina, worked for a while in a New York City garment factory, then gone into buisness with his brother-in-law, Oxman, who had a stationery store in Pleasantville. Soon after they took over, the Depression struck. Some of the wealthy people in the surrounding estates were wiped out completely, and, with a lot of time suddenly on their hands, they began to stop at the store. "That was the first we ever saw of them," Fox told me. "Before that we would only see their butler or chauffeur." They talked to Fox about the economy and about the books they were reading; Fox started to stock books. Forty years later, his is the best-stocked book, record, stationery, and toy store for miles around. A visit to Mount Kisco is for many synonymous with a visit to Fox's. The store has become as much a cultural center as Cox and Fish used to be, minus the armchairs and cuspidors.

When I was twenty-five I worked briefly at the store. My duties were to sort the paperbacks and to sweep the floor at the end of the day, and I was paid a relatively high starting salary because I had a college education. While putting the books in alphabetical order I found it difficult not to be curious about their contents, to my eventual downfall. One evening, in the second week of my employ, after I had spent too much company time on an aluminum stepladder "familiarizing myself with the stock," Cal Fox, Herman's son, came to me and told me very nervously that he really liked me and all but that he didn't think I was working out or even, for that matter, working. I said I was really sorry and would try to do better starting tomorrow, but he said no, he didn't think I should come back tomorrow.

What could I do but turn in my book of charge slips and exit gracefully? I left by the back door, walked across the parking lot, and stood on a wooden bridge watching a sluggish creek called Branch Brook flowing through the valley it had made. Empty soda cans and opalescent swirls of oil drifted under the bridge and into a thicket of reeds of Japanese bamboo. Several yards downstream a muskrat stood licking its greasy paws.

It was an evening in early June. Miasmal gases had begun to rise from the reedbeds and I could smell the produce from the empty cartons and crates in the shed behind the Finast supermarket, the fumes of a commuter train, and the blossoms of the big catalpa tree between Doris Cawley's Shell station and the movie theater. *Texas Chain-Saw Massacre* was at the movies, with *Snow White and the Seven Dwarfs* as the weekend matinee.

Just then the ten horns of the air warning system went off on the roof of the municipal building. It was six o'clock. The six deafening blasts were followed by a mellow rendition of "Rock of Ages" from the Lutheran churchbells higher up the hill, and then by the booming laughter of the barman in David's Restaurant-Bar. Swamp mosquitoes were beginning to emerge from the hollow reed stalks and old tires containing water and to swarm into the air. *Aedes canadensis, cinereus,* and *stimulans*—their bite could give you malaria or encephalitis, but has never been known to do so in Mount Kisco. A shirtless black teenager with a woolen hat rode by on a unicycle, dribbling a basketball.

I walked up Main Street, passing a policeman who was leaning against a stop sign with his hat pushed back on his head, chatting with a senior citizen. A girl who had just caught a fish in the creek came running by, grinning from ear to ear. Farther on I came on an old man hosing the suds off his twenty-year-old, immaculately kept Buick. Across the street stood the red, metallic Midnite Diner. Or rather Mid*ite Diner, since the N has been missing from its neon sign for as long as I can remember. An enormous Grand Union truck, into which you might have been able to fit the entire diner, was parked in front. I went inside, took a booth, and ordered a cup of coffee. At the counter two men, several stools away from each other, were eating hamburgers in unison. From inside the kitchen came the sound of dishes crashing to the floor, followed by an explosion in Greek. Gloria, the Puerto Rican waitress, brought my coffee, then went inside to see what had happened. I drank up, left a quarter on the table, walked to the register, dialed a toothpick, popped a mint into my mouth, and parted the double glass doors. No one there, I decided, would have been especially interested to hear that I had just been fired, but the atmosphere of indifference was benign and somehow supportive. Mount Kisco is like that.

The square in the heart of town is named for Jefferson Feigl, a Mount Kisco man killed in France on the first day of the German drive from St. Quentin, March 21, 1918. Lieutenant Feigl volunteered his services to his country while a student at Harvard and was the first American artillery officer to fall in the war. A year later his parents received his hand bag, containing a letter he had written them as he lay dying.

Dear Parents,
    I suppose you alls will be feelin' pretty low about the time this arrives. If my instructions have been carried out you'll already have received a cable telling you of the death of your one and only son. Please believe, fond parents, that I realize just what the loss means to you and what a void it's going to leave in your lives. Therefore I won't ask you to cheer up, 'cause I know it won't do any good.
    As far as I'm concerned, however, it seems as if Dame Fortune couldn't have picked a nicer or more gentlemanly manner for me to make my exit, and if it wasn't for the grief I know I'm causing you, I would be more contented now, in leaving this life, than I ever could have been while living it. If I may have a final request it is this, that any love you had for me, you'll turn it towards each other, thus filling, in some part, the gap I leave behind.
                                                        Love, Son

110

On an island in the middle of Jeff Feigl Square, surrounded by the continual flow of traffic, stands the painted zinc statue of an Indian. The Indian gazes east. His left hand grips an unstrung bow, and his left foot is slightly advanced. He wears buckskin breeches and a tiara of three upright feathers, and a cape has been tossed over his naked shouders. His long, flowing hair is anointed with pigeon droppings. The statue was donated in 1907 by long-time Mount Kisco resident and Temperance leader David Fletcher Gorham. Water used to gush from its base beneath a plaque proclaiming, "God's only beverage for man and beast." It soon became the town's best-known landmark. Travelers were told to turn left or right, or to go straight at the Indian. An oil truck knocked it from its pedestal in 1925; it was restored. According to local legend, Greta Garbo placed a wreath about its neck in 1932, and it somehow managed to appear in the seventeenth series of Ripley's *Believe It or Not*. During the turbulent 1960s it was vandalized several times and restored again. In time the Indian became known as Chief Kisco, and people started to talk as if such a chief had really existed, not realizing that dozens of identical statues had been cast at the turn of the century by the J. L. Mott Ironworks of New York City and were available by mail order. A chance discovery of the same statue in a postcard from Schenectady, New York, led Ollie Knapp, retired telephone lineman, dispatcher for the Mount Kisco fire department, and local history buff, to make an all-out search for the others. He found Chief Kisco in Barberton, Akron, Cincinnati, and Lodi, Ohio; in Ishpeming, Michigan, where he is known as "Old Ish"; and in Calhoun, Georgia, where he is called Sequoyah. The one in Cincinnati was described rather uncharitably in a WPA guidebook to Ohio as "not worth a second glance from the standpoint of art." Once when I went to South America I was charged by Knapp to verify whether a statue commemorating Atahualpa in Cuzco, Peru, was another of Mott's Indians. Unfortunately, I got to the square in which it had stood only to find that it had been lassoed by a couple of drunks three years before, and had toppled.

Jeff Feigl Square is a good place to watch the Mount Kisco Fireman's Parade. Most of the villages and hamlets in northern Westchester have a fireman's parade, but because there are four companies in Mount Kisco—the Mutuals, the Hooks, the Independents and the Fire Police—the parade of its firemen is particularly impressive. I was on hand for it in 1976, at the end of July. Having already paraded through a few villages that summer, the firemen were in top form. The main streets had been closed off. Several dozen young girls belonging to the Most Holy Trinity Drum Corps of Mamaroneck, New York, a dozen or so playing "Yankee Doodle Dandy" on piccolos, led it off. Everybody gave them a hand. Another village's chapter of the Lion's Club followed. Paunchy, gray-haired, and unknown to most of the crowd, they received a more perfunctory kind of applause. Then there was a gap in the formal procession, filled by an assortment of kids on bicycles and a vendor pushing a shopping cart decorated with gas-filled balloons. Suddenly Mount Kisco's own Ancient Fife and Drum Corps came around the corner. Sixty eighteen-inch fifes, ten base drums, and ten snares took up "The Girl I Left Behind Me." Each child wore a scarlet vest, a black tricorn hat, pants or a shirt, and sneakers. The Ancients had already appeared twice that May, once to march the Little League up to the park on opening day, and again on Memorial Day. But this was the moment for which they had been practicing in the elementary-school parking lot every Wednesday evening since Daylight Savings Time had begun, and the crowd had withheld its greatest applause for them.

Between firemen's parades are all the religious ceremonies, especially the ones connected with the Catholic church: Palm Sunday, when the congregation comes out of St. Francis of Assisi late in the morning, and the streets are filled with groups of two or three going home with the pleasant-smelling palm fronds; the funeral of a beloved villager whose casket is carried down the church steps by six American Legionnaires "who called him brother," and as the casket is slid into the limousine six other brothers in full dress raise their rifles to the sky and fire a salvo of blanks; and confirmation, when young girls in white dresses swarm around the bishop and kiss his ring as he stands in front of the church with his scepter and mitre, casting his blessing into the street. At Christmastime the churches and funeral homes on Main Street usually put out a crèche. In 1976 I counted six of them, one more imaginative and lifelike than the next. In some the figures were as big as life, in others they were made of straw. But I would have given first prize to the nativity scene in front of the Lutheran church, whose figures were *real live people,* motionless in the winter air except for the occasional plume of breath that would escape from one of them.

Mount Kisco's largest institution is the Northern Westchester Hospital. Upwards of a thousand babies are born and more than two hundred people die there each year. It is a tradition with the local merchants to give a present to the first-born child of each new year. In 1976 the lucky baby was Michael Frank Nicolosi, who came into the world at 3:33 a.m. on January 1, weighing seven pounds, six ounces. He was welcomed with five half-gallons of ice cream from Friendly's Ice-Cream Parlor, three cases of baby food from Pantry Pride, and a savings account from each of the village's seven banks. The proud mother received a twenty-pound box of no-phosphate detergent from Sears, and three free visits apiece to Thelma Hairstylists and Supersonic Car Wash. All told, the Nicolosis were showered with sixty-six presents.

Surrounding the central hospital complex an array of doctors and dentists have set up practice in smaller professional buildings and converted residences. In back of the hospital are four parallel tree-bordered streets—Boltis, Woodland, Spring, and West. It's a quiet neighborhood, not built to any set plan, but not significantly different from the architectural productions of ten thousand other American towns. Some are stucco, some brick, some wood-frame with a modest amount of gingerbread trim and maybe a shed-type garage in back. Wings, porches and other additions have been tacked on as the need arose, and every dwelling is mastered with a television aerial. The residents are Irish, Italian, and black. Families are close, but since the arrival of television, neighbors don't visit with each other or talk over the fence as much as they used to, although their children still play together in the street. The patterns of their life could be called provincial: The majority pass their lives on these four streets and are buried in the cemeteries a few hundred yards away—in Oakwood, if Protestant; in St. Francis, if Catholic, the Italians with their long Mediterranean names chiseled on the headstones. Mockingbirds, which have moved up lately from the South, are now a common sight in the cemeteries, singing in midair as they take off from the tall pines. Last spring a pair was found nesting in a hedge on West Street.

If there is anything exceptional about West Street it is that it has a lingering Italian flavor, though not as pronounced as it used to be. A few of the houses have grape arbors over the back door, and the backyards have been terraced by generations of Italians with plain or white-painted boulders. Some of the trees in the neighborhood—even Norway maples, which were planted for shade—have been severly pollarded as if they were expected to bear fruit. Come springtime, almost everyone readies a small plot for tomatoes, peppers, eggplants, zucchini squash, romaine lettuce. Later in the fall they put in escarole, which can stand the cold. Before the first frost they wrap their small fig trees in an old carpet or blanket and cover it for the winter with a garbage can. At Christmas the people at number forty-six decorate their roof with a plastic Santa Claus riding in a sleigh drawn by two reindeer whose noses light up.

"I know everybody on the street, but it's not as friendly as it is down South," said Irma Wilder, a tall, comely black woman originally from Jamaica. Still in her uniform, she had just come back from the hospital, fed her three children, and set her hair in curlers. Although she emigrated from Kingston in 1958, she has kept a lilting, Caribbean way of speaking. We sat at the kitchen table.

Irma met Bob Wilder in the Northern Westchester Hospital in 1960. She is a registered medical technologist who analyzes body fluids; Bill was in for a myocardial infarction. "We thinned out his blood to make sure it would circulate easier through the heart," she recalled.

When Bob got out, the patient and his nurse were married, and they moved to his father's place on West Street. "My father came from Rome," he told me. "He got mixed up with the Mafia and killed a man, and they gave him ten years in Sing Sing. This was a rough little town. There are very few people who really know the place, just a few old-timers.

"I was born in 1910. The Mafia was in here by the thousands. They killed one of my uncles. He gambled with them and won some money. The man that killed him never went to jail. He laid low in Chicago for ten years and then came back. The Mafia did anything that just wasn't right. Kill a man for a thousand dollars, maybe less, depending how hard up they were. The sheriff didn't bother them.

"Things got a little rough for them during the war, and most of them went out to Chicago. The big guns would pass by every once

114

in a while, but in a little burg like this there was nothing to attract them. Hell, I could tell you a lot about the Mafia, but they'd be coming to West Street. I guess a man could dig up a few skeletons in Mount Kisco if he wanted to."

Recently the Bernsteins—Stan and Marcia and their children, Judy, Cyrus, and Hilary—moved into a forty-year-old stucco Tudor house with an underhouse garage on Parkview Place, on the other side of town from West Street. It is the Bernsteins' first house; they have always lived in apartments. The move ended a process of extrication from the Bronx, up through the crowded residential rings of lower Westchester, and finally to the relative country of Mount Kisco. Parkview Place is in a solidly white middle-class neighborhood. The individual homeowner takes a great deal of pride in the appearance of his yard. Schneider, the Bernsteins' neighbor, is an ingenious man who repairs trains for Penn Central, builds grandfather clocks in his basement, and has a vegetable and flower garden that is the envy of the street. The other neighbors, who object to Max (short for Maxima), the Bernsteins' Great Dane, are not particularly friendly.

Stan, who is about forty, was born in the Bronx and grew up there. "My ideal was to live on the east side of Manhattan, but when we got married in 1956 we couldn't afford to live there, so we lived in the Bronx in a fifth-floor walkup right near the zoo. I was a sheet-metal worker involved in ductwork and air conditioning, heating, and ventilation.

"After a while we became disenchanted with the Bronx. Although we wanted the urban life, we also wanted a little nature. There was an ideal location in Fleetwood. We didn't have a car, so we used the trains, and were less than half an hour from downtown Manhattan. Out back there was a beautiful park with massive tulip trees which they have since blasted out to make the interchange between the Bronx River Parkway and the Cross-County Parkway. I would walk in the park every night rain or shine. I had a birdfeeder on every windowsill. We got them by the thousands. I grew orchids in a jerry-built greenhouse in the window.

"Finally we were kicked out because we got a dog. There were other dogs in the building, but the management didn't want any new ones. We could have taken them to court, but we decided it was time to move anyway, so we moved into the Cadillac

Apartments in Mount Vernon. Every Saturday or Sunday we would make safaris to northern Westchester, exploring the area. We drove past Fox Lane High School in Bedford and said this is where we'd like to send our kids. We saw them building Diplomat Towers in Mount Kisco and thought, here was an apartment house with a pool in the middle of the lovely country. From the apartment they showed us we could look across the tracks to this magnificent marsh, which was beautiful in the fall with all the purple loosestrife. So we took it. The first day we got there we left all the furniture in the middle of the room and went camping."

Diplomat Towers, however, did not live up to the Bernsteins' expectations. "The place began to deteriorate," Stan went on. "The management made deals for rent abatement with many of the people who lived there. Light bulbs burned out in stairwells and were not replaced, the elevator broke down almost daily, and we were constantly having to walk the six floors. The incinerator caught fire on several occasions and gave off noxious fumes. The management started renting to undesirables. They took in a known pusher and several women of questionable morals. There were an awful lot of divorced families—just a mother or father and kids who went wild. There were people who started out straight at Diplomat Towers and ended messed up.

"Things are better there now—the management has changed—but we used to go over to Diplomat all the time," William J. Nelligan, Mount Kisco's Chief of Police, told me. "Mostly for family fights, compaints of malicious mischief, or on narcotics raids. Two years ago we intercepted a twenty-five-pound bag of marijuana that was being delivered to two characters in one of the towers. They were living in a two-bedroom apartment, and their only furniture consisted of two mattresses, two early Salvation Army dressers, and a hi-fi set. Their only employment was dealing in marijuana."

Chief Nelligan was sitting at his desk in the Municipal Building. He had risen through the ranks to become, ten years ago, head of Mount Kisco's twenty-four-man force. A collection of hand guns and war medals was encased on the wall behind him. "I'm here till I retire, die, resign, or get fired," he explained. I asked him to describe the village from the law-enforcement point of view.

"Most of our complaints are family conflicts, both within and between families—people living together in close proximity. Most

116

of them are between husbands and wives. There have been a few muggings. But big crime? There isn't much of that. The armed robbery at Friendly's Ice Cream was the last one, and that was two or three years ago. We have a number of banks, but the difficulty of escaping through our congested streets and the high police presence make bank-robbing a poor risk. Of course there are your ordinary larcenies, like the one a little while back where someone stole a ring out of Grove Jewelers when the salesman's back was turned and ran off with it. Shoplifting is hard to assess. Our philosophy is to leave prosecution to the merchant's discretion. Interestingly enough, the ones who do the shoplifting are not necessarily the deprived. You go over to the kid's house and he's got everything from ice skates to a hand computer, and you try to figure out why he did it. There's been a change in the last twenty years. You used to be able to call up the parents and say, 'Joe, your son broke into a store and stole twenty-two cents,' and Joe would come down, clip the boy in the jaw, and take him home, and it would never happen again. Now they refuse to admit that it could have happened. They get defensive about it. 'You can't see him. He's in bed.' They accuse you of picking on their son."

Controlling his anger, Chief Nelligan got up and took me to see the lock-up.

"This is a high-class can," he said, showing me one of the four cells for males. "We got mattresses on the bunks, a commode, and a sink in every cell. You don't find that everywhere. The inmates are inspected every half hour. We only hold them for twenty-four hours, until they are arraigned in court the next morning. Then they're taken to the county jail." The female prisoners spend the night in a detention room, and are looked after by a matron. "There's no big problem with crime in Mount Kisco," Chief Nelligan concluded, shutting the bars of the empty cell, "thanks to me." Then, after a little pause to show he was only joking, he went on, "Actually, we have the highest concentration of criminals in northern Westchester except for Peekskill and Ossining Village, but they go and commit their crimes in other towns."

The Municipal Building of the Village of Mount Kisco—fireproof, brick, and in the Federal style—is the largest town hall in the northern part of the county. Only two of the clocks on its tower actually run, and they keep times that have no relation to Eastern Standard. In this building the mayor, the trustees, and the

117

village manager put their heads together once a week, legislate the further developments in store for Mount Kisco, and try to make sense out of what has already happened. Although an architectural review board was set up several years ago to "maintain some sort of harmony between the buildings of Mount Kisco," there isn't much it can do about the many varieties of small-town architecture which have been contributing examples of themselves there for the last hundred years. Few buildings in the village have serious architectural pretensions. The Methodist church, with its soaring spire, louvered belfry, pointed-arch window openings, and board and batten siding, is one—a good example of the Stick style or Carpenter Gothic style that flourished in the picturesque revival period between 1840 and 1860. A number of ornate Victorian residences, embellished with spacious porches, mansard roofs, turrets, pedimented dormers, flaring eaves, cast-iron porticos, porte-cocheres, projecting bays and iron finials, can be found on Captain Merritt's Hill. But most of the structures in the valley—the gas stations, stores, diners, and residences—are examples of "vernacular" architecture; they're just regular old American buildings. Lacking the self-consciousness and the formality of statelier edifices, they have an integrity and power of their own.

A few pieces of open land remain in Mount Kisco: a golf course, a reedy portion of the watershed, sixty acres of a former estate on Kisco Mountain. There are several schools of thought about this land. Some believe that Mount Kisco has already gotten out of hand, and that it might be wise to leave the last undeveloped tracts open. These people claim that the downtown streets are running double their capacity and that the old character of the village is rapidly going down the drain. They fear that Mount Kisco, with the policy of indiscriminate growth it has always followed, may be "veering toward a suicidal course."

A more powerful contingent wants to see Mount Kisco keep growing. They feel it must seek out development, or the development will go elsewhere, and the town will no longer be "the hub of northern Westchester." "If it stops, it dies," a woman at the Chamber of Commerce told me. Some would like the last open land to become the site of a big-name department store. Others dream of condominiums or a high-rise parking garage. Too many residents, the "town house" faction argues, are now renters of apartments. Mount Kisco needs to get back to the owner; he would do more for the town. As for the traffic problems additional people might create, Henry Kensing, the Mayor, did not seem worried. "Normally," he said, "it takes five minutes to get from one end of town to the other.

9 *The Days of the Big Houses*

From about 1880 to 1940, a few people lived in a degree of material splendor that will never be known in Westchester again. The rich lived in mansions designed by the best architects, filled with the best art from Europe and the Far East, and looking out at the best views across carefully landscaped expanses of their own property.

James Sutton built one of the first big houses. He married the only daughter of R. H. Macy, which brought him a great fortune. In the 1880s he bought several hundred acres in Bedford and hired a well-known French architect to build a big house for him on the top of a hill. The long *allée* leading up to it was planted with young maples that have since grown into magnificent specimens. The entire hillside was converted into a spacious, rolling lawn of perhaps twelve acres that was maintained by a horse-drawn mower. The horses wore special leather boots to prevent them from marking up the turf.

But the building of the house seemed to take forever. At last one June morning, the architect came to the Suttons, presented them with a key, and told them to meet him in the front hall at nine o'clock the following morning. The house was ready. At nine the Suttons put the key in the front door, opened it, and were greeted by the sight of the architect hanging by his neck in the stairwell. "Despite this rather gruesome beginning," their neighbor, Gustavus Kirby, wrote in his memoirs, "the Suttons lived in their home for many years."

They were lovely days in many ways. The big houses were filled with an endless round of great balls and house parties. There were charades and recitals in the music room, garden parties, and croquet on the lawn. The ladies all went calling. Whenever a newcomer moved in everybody would get dressed up in their best clothes and present their calling cards, leaving the coachmen to pace up and down outside. The sporty group rode in the Fairfield and Westchester hounds.

Coaching enjoyed a vogue until the end of the twenties. Good conversation was to be had. There was an intellectual group that was the Bedford equivalent of the Boston Brahmins. Henry Marquand, an art historian who wrote on all sorts of subjects, lived on one of the hills, and Edith Wharton often came to stay. Charles Scribner, who had started a publishing house, was gregarious and often brought his authors out for the weekend. The sporty group tended to be rather stuffy, the intellectual group eccentric.

Things were more formal then, of course. In fact, the dress was often uncomfortable. Women poured their bodies into corsets that made them look like hourglasses. People ate too much and didn't exercise enough. And the children had nice times as well. Family outings—picnics, boating, hikes—were more common than they are today. When the automobile arrived the great Sunday occupation was to pile into one's glossy new electric and go for a drive. The kids would play roadside cribbage. A cow was worth ten, a horse fifteen, a goat twenty, and a black sheep won the game.

Labor was easy to get and every house had a big staff. There were coal-burning stoves in the laundry on which the kitchenmaids would heat up the irons, and big tables on which they would iron. One house had a Finnish cook who liked to stay alone and talk to the animals. She had her skis at the kitchen door and would step into them to get the groceries. In the village they called her the Flying Finn. A Mr. Miller, the butcher, killed his own beef and delivered it personally. The merchants didn't say, "Have a nice day," in those days as they do now.

Bedford was changing from a farming community into a commuting town, but many of the men who worked in the city still made a fairly elaborate attempt at farming. They had cows and pigs and chickens and a greenhouse and smoked the hams. They relaxed by competing with each other over the size of their melons. One of the more successful attempts was Charles Darlington's Rock Gate Farm. Dairy farming had become a losing proposition after the First World War, but Darlington tried to turn back the clock and held on till the Second World War. After that the only hands he could get were drifters. His milk was famous and especially good for babies. A woman from Bedford, touring Europe one year, was startled in her pensione in Florence to be served Rock Gate Farm milk for her *café latte.* You still occasionally find Rock Gate Farm bottles in the woods.

It was also a period of cultural advancement. Miss Helen Clay Frick, the daughter of the Pittsburgh steel baron, continued to collect art for her father's museum on Fifth Avenue, while living in strict privacy and relative simplicity in a farmhouse in Bedford. She and others of a more solitary bent took a great interest in the local birds and wildflowers. Miss Eloise Payne Lucquer painted exquisite watercolors of wildflowers, and a speech she gave on the pulse family was considered so good that it was privately printed and distributed among her friends. She and her friend Miss Delia Marble started a native plant garden in the Ward Pound Ridge Reservation and organized "farmerettes" to milk the cows and harvest the vegetables while the men were off in the great war. The Bedford Agassiz Society was started for the study of local natural history. Its members prepared a herbarium of the local flora which has since unfortunately disappeared. A magazine called *Westchester Countryside,* devoted to celebrating and enumerating the local flora and fauna, lasted from 1936 to 1937.

There was an even greater interest in gardening and plants were brought in from all over the world. Some of them escaped and are now growing wild in the woods. Pink dogwood was introduced about 1917; euonymus came a bit later. Pachysandra, myrtle, banks of violet, and other groundcovers came in the late thirties when it became difficult to get a man to cut the lawn. The Marquand house was decorated with wisteria brought over from Japan. The Bechtels' rose garden was a breathtaking array of hybrids in a maze of sculpted hedges. Bedford boasted some of the most fabulous gardens in the country, and it still does. There were Italian gardens, oriental gardens, romantic gardens, informal English gardens, perennial gardens with marvelous delphiniums. The first chapter of the Garden Club of America was started in Bedford in 1938. Christina Rainsford wrote a poem called "Imperfect Paradise" about her garden. The meter and rhyme scheme are that of "The Rubaiyat of Omar Khayam."

> Wake, for the coffee bubbles in the pot,
> The egg is waiting and the toast is hot.
> This is no day for lingering in bed,
> We must be up and dig our garden plot.
>
> Sometimes I think that never flower grows
> That blooms as long or smells as sweet as those
> So glowingly portrayed in catalogues.
> Why do ours never look the same? Who knows.
>
> Eager to learn I zealously frequent
> The Garden Club and hear great argument
> Concerning pesticides but oftentimes
> Come out as ignorant as when I went.
>
> Ah, my beloved, if our garden seed
> Could grow and bloom with never any weed,
> With never any blight or worm or slug
> Our garden would be paradise indeed.

It was, for the few who had the wealth and the leisure and the land to get the most out of it, an idyllic life. But in the end the outside world caught up with it. The days of big houses ended with the Second World War. Maids disappeared, and they never appeared again. They got better jobs in factories and offices. A wave of blacks came but not in sufficient numbers to replace the Irish and the Italians who had been the maids, butlers, gardeners, chauffeurs, and nannies.

The fortunes made in the nineteenth century were divided and divided again. What with the soaring property taxes, the shortage of domestics, and the rising cost of heating fuel, people just couldn't pay the freight on a big house anymore. Estates built by senior executives were broken up into junior estates and sold to junior executives, or turned over to various organizations to be run as nature sanctuaries.

The houses themselves were hard to unload. I can think of a dozen right now that are vacant on the hilltops of Bedford. Some of them have been on the market for years and haven't drawn so much as a nibble. I walked through the old Glass estate in Mount Kisco recently. It was depressing to see what had become of the place: the cement coming apart in the empty pools, the poolhouse windows smashed, the greenhouse windows gone, the delicious apples in the orchards just rotting beneath the trees.

In a few parts of the north-county the big houses are still inhabited by their original owners, and the nineteenth and twentieth centuries seem checkerboarded. In the natural course of things, the men usually die first, and some of the most magnificent old dwellings are inhabited by lone women of advanced age who lost their husbands ten, twenty, even forty years ago. There is a saying in Bedford that thirty rich widows run the town, and it does seem at times as if a subtle matriarchy were in effect. A formidable woman named Mrs. Lathrop Colgate was the arbiter of taste there for forty years. She was the Queen of Bedford, a great character, very civilized and an honorary fireman. If there was something of which she did not approve, she would simply buy it. I can remember a boisterous working-class dive on Route 22 called the Wigwam suddenly going out of business in the fifties. Mrs. Colgate cleaned up several other dens of iniquity along 22, and to this day there isn't a decent bar in Bedford Village, although the woman has been dead for more than fifteen years.

The power of these dowagers is not to be underestimated. It is largely they who keep alive the churches, schools, hospitals, and fire departments in Bedford, and if some ignorant bungler in White Plains has decided to run a road through one of their estates, he soon gets word that he'll have to figure out another route. Many of these women are quite eccentric. There is one who leans over the front seat and presses the horn with the end of her cane if her chauffeur isn't driving fast enough. Another has actually been known to take her cane to someone who did not

125

amuse her. A third, to whom I was often taken to tea as a child, had so many prejudices that I had to write them on the inside of my shirt cuff to make sure I wouldn't offend her. A fourth's daily routine involves the consumption of three martinis—one before lunch, and two before dinner. One evening some burglars burst into her living room at the cocktail hour. Without batting an eyelash she insisted that they have a drink with her while she finished her martini. For half an hour her conversation held the crooks in awe. She then proceeded to show them around, pointing out the *objets* that were of personal value and not to be taken. She told the thieves they could help themselves to the rest, which they did.

At the end of the nineteenth century the big houses were built in a number of styles. There was a turning away from Victorian Gothic to a Colonial simplicity, of which the Van Cortlandt house on Guard Hill Road in Bedford, a farmhouse that was expanded and rebuilt by Stanford White, is a good example. In the early 1920s "bastard Norman" Newport and Narragansett houses, half shingle, half stone, became popular. After 1914 everybody built French châteaux and in the twenties they went in for the Tudor look. A few Regency houses went up too, but the handsomest big houses were Georgian.

The house of Dr. Robert L. Patterson is a large Georgian, elegant in the purity and simplicity of its lines. It was designed by the firm of Delano & Aldrich and built over 1905 and 1906 for William Sloane, whose father had built up a family rug and furniture business into an enormously successful New York department store. The house in Mount Kisco was meant as a surprise for his wife. She never saw it until it was completed and fully furnished. The Sloanes' daughter Margaret became Mrs. Patterson. She was born in the house, and still lives there a good deal of the year. Inside the house are framed signatures of all the presidents of the United States. Outside is one of the few grass tennis courts still maintained in Westchester. The lines are powdered with chalk and the bounce is low, fast, and unpredictable. In a nearby coop are the Pattersons' peacocks. Every time a ball smacks the net the peacocks let out a squawk that can be heard in the valley below. The tennis court was responsible for bringing Dr. Patterson and his wife together. He was a young doctor from Georgia doing his residency in orthopedics at Presbyterian Hospital in New York. During a weekend visit to his uncle, who lived nearby, Patterson was asked to the Sloanes' for a game of tennis. Margaret, in a long skirt, slipped and scraped her knee. The young doctor offered to examine it. "I took one look at her knee and that was that," Dr. Patterson said.

"It was a working farm," his wife said. Her face became luminous as she spoke of her childhood. "We milked cows, kept pigs, chickens, cut ice and stored it in an ice house. There were two root cellars—one for potatoes and the other for apples. Mrs. Hughes used to bong the gong for lunch. She hit it with a sledgehammer. Our working horses were Belgian. They were sorrel-colored with white manes and fetlocks and absolutely enormous. They plowed and they reaped and they hayed and they ran away and busted down the grapes once. I used to drive my high-stepping hackneys down the station. I had horses way into the thirties. We had a big old Pierce Arrow, too, with isinglass windows and a canvas top you had to buckle on and off.

"In the beginning there was no one here. Then the Meyers and the Cooks and the Strauses came and built their houses. Eugene Meyer was my father's classmate in 1895. He started the Washington *Post*. His sister married Alfred Cook. Jesse Straus was the ambassador to France. They were very high-caliber people, who kept to themselves. Of course, they couldn't get into the country club. By 1937, when Dewitt and Lila Wallace (who founded the *Reader's Digest*) built their house here, it was hilltopper country. My mother broke through that hilltopper thing. She couldn't stand hearing all that social talk. I think that hilltopper thing was just terrible."

But the Tuckers had the greatest estate of all in the Bedford area. Three quarters of a century ago, Carll and Marcia Tucker bought all the land enclosed by three roads—something like five hundred acres—and hired Frederick Law Olmsted's architectural firm to design an estate for them. Olmsted was the best there was. He had been responsible for Central Park in New York and had already done a few jobs in Westchester. He had designed the broad main street of the new hamlet of Katonah, after the old one was flooded over by the reservoir. For the Tuckers he called upon the Tudor, Norman, Gothic, and Romanesque styles and several others to give them Penwood—a group of weighty stone structures whose last detail, whose every crenelation and machicolation, would evoke the best traditions of European culture.

Carll Tucker's family had published a magazine called *The Country Gentleman*, and he was himself what was known as a gentleman of leisure. He married Marcia Brady, whose father, Anthony, was one of Thomas Edison's business partners and left at his death one of the largest personal fortunes that had ever been accumulated. It was divided nine ways. Tucker managed his wife's money very well. Besides Penwood, they had residences on Park Avenue and at Hobe Sound and a huge schooner called the *Migrant* which was one of the largest private vessels afloat until it was commandeered by the Navy in the Second-World War.

Carll died a number of years ago, and Marcia died in 1976 in her nineties. The main house at Penwood has been closed and empty for about twelve years. The Tuckers' son, Carll Jr., became active in local affairs around Mount Kisco, founding a newspaper called the *Patent Trader*. Near Penwood he built an enormous French château on the scale of the mansions of the tens and the twenties but the year it was finished, 1968, he died of a heart attack at the age of forty-six. His son, Carll III, used to invite me to play squash in the court at Penwood until he moved into the city, where he is now the chairman and editor of the *Saturday Review*. The Tuckers are one of the few intact dynasties, whose status in Westchester is eclipsed only by the Rockefellers of Pocantico Hills. Several years ago, young Carll commissioned the architect Robert Venturi to build him a new house. The Tucker house, as it is already being called, looks very much like a large birdhouse. According to the architectural historian Vincent Scollay, it represents "the ultimate reaction to Frank Lloyd Wright, the reassertion of the vertical." Now that most of the level ground in Westchester has been spoken for, we are probably going to see a lot of vertical housing on the slopes, woodland dwellings with the upper story in the canopy of the forest, of which the Tucker house will be a classic example.

Shortly after the house was ready, I found Carll at home. Outside two men with shovels were talking to each other in Italian while putting the finishing touches on what would be the front lawn. Inside, Carll was supervising the hanging of his pictures. Most of them were old prints of European landscapes, and there was a small oil in the bedroom by an Impressionist and an Elizabethan portrait in the dining room, where we sat and talked for a while about growing up at Penwood, and what the move to a newer and smaller Tucker house represented. "Properties are smaller," he declared. "Wealth has become anonymous. When I was growing up everybody knew my name. All the shop people. It's no longer the case, which is fine by me. We lived on such a huge place far away from everybody. I was alone but had lots to do. Horses and dogs were my playmates. I grew up in an adult world, surrounded by grooms and maids. At Yale I was never much of a hail-fellow-well-met. I was clumsy socially, and didn't know how to deal with my contemporaries until they became adults themselves. My way of keeping up the family tradition was to be an achiever—writer, musician, top of the class. My father chose to start a newspaper in the town where he had grown up, which was some kind of masochism. He wanted to prove himself not one of the idle rich. Make it in your own backyard. Go to people you had regarded as servants and ask for their advertising." Carll went into the bedroom and changed into his whites. He was off to the country club. "Tennis is an important part of my life," he said. "I try to play some racket sport as often as I can."

A few months later I met Carll at Penwood. He had become engaged and his fiancée was as curious as I to see the inside of the main house. I had only been in the squash building and the greenhouse whose three long wings were maintained by a family of Italians who kept Carll's grandmother supplied with flowers throughout the year. The main house had been built from 1912 to 1920, with an interruption while the First World War was being fought. Sicilian stonemasons had been imported for the job. "The inner courtyard is Tudor, around the outer part is Romanesque, and the inside in Gothic," Carll explained. The kitchen took up several rooms, in which only the great cast-iron ranges with their metal hoods and the long zinc sinks remained. In the dining room were a magnificent Delft fireplace and a dozen or so high-backed chairs with the Tucker crest (a lion's paw holding up the motto NIHIL DESPERANDUM). Baroque Italian frescoes showing pastoral maidens and shepherds romping in a misty hillscape paneled the walls. Our footsteps echoed down the long dark corridor of a hallway lined with stone arches that might have come from some Gothic cathedral. "The house isn't known for its lightness," Carll said as we felt our way into the study. Several shelves were still filled with leather-bound sets of Thackeray and George Eliot, but the extensive ornithological collection had gone to Cornell. Twelve servants had been attached to the house. They were quartered over the kitchen in small rooms whose size depended on their importance. The butler had been given the biggest one.

10 *Crumbling Strata*

One afternoon, for perhaps the forty thousandth time, I drove into Bedford Village. The place has changed little, at least physically, since I grew up there twenty years ago. There were the triangular green with the flagpole in the center and the sign proclaiming in florid green italics: BEDFORD GREEN PART OF A COMMON LAID OUT IN 1681 FOR GRAZING CATTLE, HORSES, AND SWINE. There was the old white cottage with moss-covered shingles that may have harbored a Tory sympathizer and thus escaped burning during the Revolution; since several other houses also make the claim, no one is quite sure. There were the little Doric office and the gambrel-roofed courthouse in which the supervisors of Westchester met every other year until 1870; the old cannon over which the male dogs of the neighborhood ritually raise their legs; the lone brick apartment house that a developer managed to sneak in during the 1940s when most of the town board was on vacation. There was the movie theater, still run by Mrs. Meade. We called her mean old Mrs. Meade because she didn't take kindly to kids who stole in through the exits.

I first stopped at the Woods to pick up a book. Captain Gerard

131

Wood and his marvelously vague and kindly wife Frances live on the Pound Ridge Road in the ancestral Wood home. He is descended from one of the twenty-two Puritan families who came to Bedford from Stamford, Connecticut, in 1680, relieving the Tanketeke Indians of their land for £44 worth of merchandise. Their seventeen-room mansion was erected in 1784 by the captain's great-great-grandfather and renovated a century later by his grandfather, a Victorian architect. Portraits of the family and a collection of clocks and Empire furniture fill the downstairs rooms.

The Woods gave me my first job. I was fifteen and they had just returned from two years in Hawaii, where they'd been looking after Frances's mother during her terminal illness. When they got back to the house in Bedford, there was a lot of cleaning and dusting and airing to be done. They had left for Hawaii right after a large dinner party, leaving unwashed the pots and pans involved in its production. No amount of elbowgrease could have possibly restored the wares to respectability, and the wages Frances paid me to clean them could have bought a whole new set of pots and pans; but Frances felt it was high time I had a job.

I asked about her son Hadden, who had prospected for gold and emeralds in the Ecuadorian Amazon for several years and was now trying a third time to cross the Atlantic in a balloon. It was he who had flown me over Westchester.

After tea with the Woods I had a few drinks with Beatrice Monroe. Aunt Beat, as I have always called her, lives in a big old colonial across the street from the house in which I grew up. She spent fifty-two years in real estate. In her youth she commuted to Manhattan on a motorcycle and sold a good part of the island to people who wanted to put up skyscrapers. She made her contacts on the golf course. Her father, Henry R. Loundsberry, founded the Bedford Golf and Tennis Club in 1898, and was one of the first golfers in the country. His clubs were made in Scotland. When Beat was sixteen she had a national handicap of three. Beat is not a teetotaler, and she enjoys a good joke. One time she called my father when he was president of the Bedford Audubon Society and told him to come over and take a look at a flock of flamingos that had landed in her backyard. Let me know if they're there in the morning, he said to her.

When they were children Aunt Beat played with Captain Wood.

132

He still has a piece missing from his left ear from the time she winged a stone at him. She also bobsledded with Junior Hockley. He'd push, she'd steer, and they'd shoot straight down the middle of 22, there was so little traffic then. William P. Hockley, seventy, lives just out of the hamlet, a quarter of a mile from Beat's house. He sharpens skates and fixes lawnmowers. His grandfather, whose name was also William P. Hockley, was the village blacksmith. "I was born right in this house," he told me as he wheeled my four-blade Jacobsen out of his shed that evening. "I had an aunt and she lived to be ninety-four and her mind was clear right up to the end, and she told me that this house and the little house on the golf course were the two houses that weren't burned by the British." The burning of Bedford was the worst debacle the hamlet had ever known. "The inhabitants were left destitute and homeless to devise whatever rude shelters they could," according to a booklet published by the historical society.

"My grandfather had the first car in Bedford and that must have been around 1900, I imagine," Hockley went on. He took me into his office and fished out a tintype of the "locomobile" from one of the many cluttered compartments in his desk. "Here's an old Mount Kisco *Recorder*. January 14, 1898. Handle it with care. It'll come apart on you. This old paper's seen better days":

Excitement still continues over the report that Mr. Wm. P. Hockley has purchased a steam traction engine with the object of hauling quartz from the quarry here to Bedford Station.
Objections:
Apart from the damage it would cause in runaway horses, etc., it would shake our small bridges all to pieces . . . While we would not like to interfere in any way with any progressive enterprise, we certainly would not tolerate a public nuisance, or anything that would destroy our public roads or plunge the town in enormous expense for solid stone bridges.

"Well, they couldn't stop him," Hockley said, shooting me a mischievous look from under the vizor of the faded gray cap I've never seen him remove.

The amazing thing about Bedford Village is how effectively it has resisted change. One would expect this of a provincial village in the Midi, or a staid town in Vermont, but with New York City—

surely one of the most volatile spots on earth—only forty-three miles away (the distance is chiseled on an ancient milestone in the middle of the hamlet), Bedford Village is really extraordinary. People who decide to live in Bedford generally stay, as opposed to Chappaqua, where the average occupancy of a house is about two years. They have a sense of belonging to something. As Donald Marshal, the town historian, put it: "The knowledge that the community has been here for centuries, like the Bedford Oak, gives as much of a sense of security as can be expected to be found today."

The old oak on the corner of Hook Road and Cantitoe Street, a mile from the hamlet, is the chief contender for the oldest tree in the county. Increment borings have put its age at over five hundred years. My students once took its measurements. It took nine of them to girdle it with their joined hands. Others spaced off its span—one hundred and twenty feet—and determined, by comparing its shadow with that of an upright, three-foot broom handle, that it was ninety feet high. With its long, sinuous limbs it looks more like a live oak in Georgia than a white oak in New York. You'd expect it to be draped with Spanish moss and festooned with bromeliads, but only epiphytic moss and a plant that looks like mistletoe have sprouted in the main crotch. It used to be called the Woodcock Oak because it belonged to a man by that name. At the turn of the century a prosperous farmer named Clarence Whitman bought it, and would make his children remove their hats whenever they rode by. A few years ago it was almost destroyed when a fuel truck caught fire beneath it. Just recently the neighboring field was sold to a developer who, unmoved by the entreaties of the townspeople, promptly built an ugly speculation house a hundred yards away. The tree is said to have a ghost called Abigail. If you stand in front of it in the light of a full moon and say, "Abigail, Abigail," she is supposed to appear. The Suburban Tree Company of Bedford Village has the enormous responsibility of keeping the oak alive, which they do by routine pruning, spraying, and deep-root feeding. If the oak ever died, there would be hell to pay.

The social strata of Bedford are easily identified. With a little practice you can tell immediately whether a person is a townie, a merchant, a middle-class burger, a nouveau, a hilltopper or a misfit. During the tumultuous 1960s, when the strata seemed on

134

the point of collapsing, there was a mass defection of youth from the upper strata. But for all the testing the structure survived, and now a new crowd of rather intimidating young women strides to the post office in velvet riding helmets, in tennis dresses and golf cleats. Each time I pass through the hamlet it seems less real, almost like a movie set. And occasionally one does see a housewife on the green, testifying before a television camera to the virtues of a certain brand of maple syrup. Several years ago my brother, who prides himself on looking like a local, was accosted by a man in a beret who offered him five dollars to walk again from his car to the post office. The footage became part of *The Valley of the Dolls*.

The son of the local exterminator, Gary Powell, is in the septic-tank business and doing pretty well for himself: His wife just had their second child, he's got his own business with several men under him, and he's Assistant Chief in the Bedford Village Fire Department. "After I got out of the service," he told me, "I worked for a guy who went under." Gradually Gary started to build up one of the thirty-one septic services in the county, buying out two others when the owners retired. "You buy the good will, the first crack," he explained. Since he took over Michael Murphy's lucrative business, he now pumps out the sewers on most of the estates in Bedford, and his red "honey wagon" is a familiar sight in town. "If I don't make three hundred a day, I don't break even. I work for nine hundred people a year, and there's maybe fifteen hundred houses in Bedford, so I get to see them all at one time or another. I bet you I got a year's work lined up here." We were leaning on the sliding glass door of the firehouse, watching women go by. "A lot of people in their thirties are mortgaged to the hilt. They live in the speculation houses and want two cars in the garage and four kids running around and to drink gin and tonic all day Saturday. I've had more trouble collecting from these types than from the estate people. Don't knock the hilltoppers. They're my bread."

At twenty-eight Gary is probably the youngest assistant chief in the county. "The new people take it for granted, but they don't realize that it's a volunteer fire department. We pay for everything, buy our own uniforms, even our own beer." The Bedford Village Fire Department has the reputation of being a private club for the townies and the merchants, so I asked him if anybody could join. He looked at me, then said, "The only stipulation is you got to live in the district." There are a few doctors and lawyers, but the majority of the firemen "deal in the services." Like the upper class who don't care to socialize with the fire department, they prefer their own crowd. "The crowd that is here mostly joined after World War II so they're mostly in their fifties now," Gary went on. "In fact we're putting on a little drive. Any new faces are quite welcome here." Gary put a quarter into a machine and took out a bottle of Genessee beer and handed it to me. Down in the basement there is a bowling alley whose four lanes are rented out at night to several men's and women's leagues. Upstairs there are three pool tables, a large sailfish, and a room full of the trophies the fire department has won for the best appearance in the parades that go on around the county from Memorial Day through September.

The department has four pumpers, an ambulance, a light rescue truck, and an aluminum boat used to rescue stranded flood victims and people who fall through the ice. "We have our own scuba team, consists of about six people. The town doesn't have any hydrants. We have a truck with one mile of hose. Use streams, ponds, and swimming pools. Carry fourteen hundred gallons with us.

"The fire phone will ring eleven spots. Any one of the three chiefs pushes a button which sounds an alarm in every one of the sixty-five active firemen's homes. Then they tell you where the fire is and the four horns go off on the roof for those who aren't at home. Last year we put out eighty-five, ninety fires. But we do more ambulance. The heart is the biggest thing now. We got hospital trained men—AMTs. We must do over a hundred ambulance a year."

Rippowam, the local day school. Focal point of the young upper-class set and the set that aspires to the upper class. Forming, along with the country club and the Episcopal church, the so-called "holy Trinity" of Bedford's socially prominent. First step in the traditional progression to prep school and then Harvard, Princeton, or Yale. An interesting assortment of people on the faculty. Some have social background but couldn't hack the pressures of Wall Street. Many are dedicated career teachers who have put in several decades here, patiently infusing the children of the rich and well-born with the rudiments of an education. I attended Rip in the late 1950s. A high point was dancing class on Wednesday afternoon, where we learned from a lithe woman in tights named Miss Stephanie how to do the rhumba, lindy, tango, waltz, foxtrot, Mexican shuffle, and bunny-hop. Few of us would have the chance to demonstrate our mastery of these steps in later life, but getting them down was nevertheless considered a necessary part of our training as young ladies and gentlemen.

"I've been a teacher for thirty-six years," one of my old teachers said one evening as we settled onto his living-room couch. "I came from a mill town in Massachusetts and I grew up thinking I was going to play baseball. In 1938 I spent half a season in 'the bushes,' pitching for the Canton Red Sox—a farm team of the Boston Sox. But I got chips in my elbow, and that was that."

Then he joined the Navy, spending an eighteen-month tour on the aircraft carrier *Essex* as a landing signal officer. "I guess that was when I started teaching. I was teaching them how to come aboard." He still uses Navy lingo like "Now hear this" in the classroom, and he has reenacted in the classroom the dramas of the Pacific Theater for generations of Bedford schoolchildren. I remember a particularly gory story about how a kamikaze plane crashed on the deck and he bent down to pick up what he thought was a piece of the plane and realized it was a piece of the pilot. For the last two years he's been working on a nine-foot balsa model of the ship. He is about halfway done. "It would take me a month if I put in straight eight-hour days. I only work on it when I get the urge." In his workroom are completed models of ocean liners, blimps, Model T's, autos, clipper ships, World War II fighters, dive bombers, TBDs (torpedo planes), carrier planes with folded wings, trains, and a couple of World War I biplanes. In his son's room is an enormous exact replica in balsa of the *Saratoga*. "I built her as she was in twenty-eight when she was launched." His two sons are grown up now, both teachers, one of disabled children, the other of Navy ensigns.

After the war was over he heard that a school called Rippowam was looking for a sixth-grade teacher. He and his wife drove up to Bedford and found that it was just like the town in New Jersey where she had grown up. It was the first private school he had ever taught at. "We were impressed with the self-confidence of the people, and their children were a lot different from down in the public schools. The people were impressed with their success. They were established, settled. Most of them had large staffs: gardeners, two people in the house, a chauffeur. When we came here the kids were being chauffeured over in big Lincolns and La Salles. It was easier in those days from the teacher's point of view because the kids were self-motivated. They knew which boarding schools they were going to because their dad went there.

"The parents are younger now," he went on; "on their way up. We used to have the presidents. Now we have the general managers. There's more pressure on them. There are a lot more divorces now."

Roland Rudd has been the organist at St. Matthew's since 1944. It's a beautiful old country church where King James's English can still be heard. Among the rector's traditional duties is the blessing of the bassets before they go to the hunt. At six o'clock the churchbell peals, reminding everyone within earshot that it is time for cocktails.

Rudd has worked under four rectors. The first, Arthur Ketchum, has not been forgotten by the community. "He was the holiest man I will ever meet," a woman in his parish told me. "He had the ability to open up even the most reserved people," Rudd said as we sat in the vestry one afternoon. "He was a rare conversationalist who never used a note in the pulpit and went on and on in the most inspiring manner." He never drove, never married, and died in his eighties in the late nineteen-fifties, leaving behind several beautiful plays in the manner of Yeats and Synge. There were special places in the garden around the rectory where he liked to sit and write poetry. His poems are remarkable for their lyrical clarity and their feeling for nature:

I wish you would come this way again, Johnnie Appleseed,
For the peepers are shrilling through the dusk
And the swamp-maples are tipped with fire
And it's planting time . . .

I remember his visit when I was nine and hospitalized with a suspected ruptured spleen. Placing his fine, old liver-spotted hands on my head, he spoke to me in a wonderfully consoling voice, then took out a deck of cards and proceeded to teach me how to play canasta.

"John Harper came at a time when church–going was on the increase," Rudd continued. "It was after the Korean War. Young people were attracted to him. He would put you on an instantaneous first-name basis. His way was very different from that of Mr. Ketchum, and it annoyed some of the older ladies. His sermons were clear and strong but some thought he never saw his points to their proper conclusions. His parishioners felt that he was very warm and gentle, but those who worked for him saw him in a different way. He was a very complicated person, hard to work for. Sometimes he could be very hurtful. He pulled his punches in a very self-seeking way." Harper is now the rector of a prestigious church in Washington, across Pennsylvania Avenue from the White House.

"Mr. Hargate has been here almost fifteen years. He is marvelous on a one-to-one basis, and in many ways the best rector to work for. He is a traditionalist, but he is fair and gives you responsibility. Funerals are his best service. He's looking at you and really connecting."

Although I was confirmed at St. Matthew's I have not set foot in the church in years. The last time I was there—I couldn't have been more than thirteen—Mr. Rudd struck up one of my favorite hymns and I started to belt it out and everybody turned around and glared at me. My mother tugged at my sleeve trying to get me to stop singing so loud and whispering anxiously in French, *"Tout le monde nous regarde."*

"Congregational singing *is* inhibited," Rudd admitted, "although it's stronger here than in most Protestant churches. I sometimes use the old Toscanini trick of speeding it up a bit. In fact at times they've been left a bit breathless."

If it isn't to sing, why *do* the people come to church? "That," said Rudd after a long pause, "is a very good question. The Christian doctrine is repeated and spoken but the social thing—seeing your friends, et cetera—this has to be the important thing. For a number of people the repetition of the prayer and meditation don't sink in very deeply. No, it's the social thing. You go to this church to be on the right side of the tracks. I'm sure you've heard Bedford referred to as an oasis—something away from the total life. The erection of stone walls around a group of people only

139

hurts the people who've done it. They're not experiencing the total thing at all."

Between services, choir practices, and piano lessons, Rudd has a lot of time on his hands. On his free mornings he likes to walk the streets of Mount Kisco. "I make various stops giving some of my bad puns to the shopkeepers." Most of them are plays on his name, like "rough and ruddy." In Bedford Village members of the upper stratum don't usually say hello to servants of the community like Rudd. "I'm used to it," Rudd said philosophically. "The various slights that hurt me in my early years don't hurt me anymore. I *like* many of the people who don't recognize me when I pass."

No one in Bedford is really poor, except in the low-rent pockets of Bedford Hills and Mount Kisco. Most citizens have met with enough success to own their own houses. The rich live in big houses which they deprecate as "cottages," while the middle class inhabits Farms, Manors, and Estates which are actually closely juxtaposed ranch or colonial "speculation" houses. Many of the actual farms, manors, and estates in Bedford are being chopped up into Farms, Manors, and Estates, and the middle class has been enjoying a population explosion. The habitat is instantly familiar: the no-nonsense houses, the manicured lawn, the two cars in the driveway, one of which is usually a ranch wagon. The people who live in it work mainly for large corporations within the county—IBM, General Foods, American Can. They are respectable, gregarious, and for the most part transient. In a few years most of them will be transferred by the company to similar habitats in other parts of the country. On Saturday night in the summertime the air in the subdivisions is heavy with the smell of cut grass and barbecued hamburger.

Bedford Estates is twelve years old. It's middle-class country—tight rows of cedar-shake colonials and split-levels but some attempt has been made to make the houses different from one another.

The Maitlands, who live on a circle at the end of a cul-de-sac called Robin Hood Road, were the first family on the street. Other streets are Richard's Court, Nottingham Road, Friar's Close, and Locksley Lane. "People say, oh, you live over in Sherwood Forest," Ed Maitland told me. "Our road is very neighbory," his daughter

Maureen wrote for me in a science paper. "The bird life is very high. We have several bird houses in our backyard and only one of them has a vacancy." Of the twelve families on Robin Hood Road, eight have been there from the beginning. A number of the men commute to the city: One works on the stock exchange, two are in advertising, one with a cosmetics company. Another works locally the telephone company, and still another with IBM.

Ed Maitland is senior vice-president of an advertising agency in New York City that specializes in the promotion of pharmaceuticals. The Maitlands came up from Bethpage, Long Island. "Concrete and traffic chased us off the island," she explained. "We had outgrown our house," Ed added. "We wanted a bigger house, we wanted more property, we wanted tall timber. This was all virgin forest before the houses were built," he said, motioning toward the remaining oaks and maples visible at the back of his half-acre lot through sliding glass doors. "Our number-one criterion for buying into this community was to have playmates for the kids. The cul-de-sac was safe, and we could see that the other people who were looking at the model homes had children. We lead a child-oriented existence. We want to be able to see our kids over the supper table. Maybe we're selfish about it, but we want them home."

In the summer the Maitlands spend a lot of time on their patio. "We have regular outdoor living," Ed said. "I spend about fifty percent of my free time keeping the place up. We were sort of spoiled in Long Island. There you threw down the seeds and they grew. Here you really have to work to make the place look nice. I have probably rebuilt my lawn fifteen times, and that gets to you after a while, but we're not unique. Every one of us here in Sherwood Forest makes an extraordinary effort to beautify and keep up their property.

"We're very fond of this town," he concluded. "If we move somewhere it will probably be within Bedford."

Dick and Carol Wallace, who describe themselves as the "new bland," live in a single-level modular ranch house with a cathedral ceiling. The house came in three sections which were built in Pennsylvania, delivered in oversized trailers, and put together in August of 1973 on a wooded, three-acre lot outside of Bedford Village. The Wallaces have a minimum of equity tied up in the house. "We caretake it for the bank," John joked. He is, at twenty-eight, a corporate lawyer who defends his company against race, sex, and age discrimination charges from disgruntled employees and ex-employees. When they moved up from North White Plains a few years ago they hardly knew a soul. Down the road from them is Memorial Field, the Bedford Village park. "I started going down to the pool at Memorial Field, meeting ladies and playing tennis," Carol said, recalling their first summer there. "You know, all those decadent things that housewives do in the summertime. Through the gang at Memorial Field I was introduced to the Newcomers Club. Newcomers is a forum for meeting people. It's basically for the wives in the subdivisions. They get together once a week, play bridge, and talk about books like *The French Lieutenant's Woman*. They're youngish—in their late twenties to early forties. Most of them are transferred every five years and are professionally outgoing and used to making their way in new situations. I suppose you'd call them corporate transplants. In transient communities like the Farms [Bedford Farms, a nearby subdivision] people are moving in and out all the time and there's a committee that's on the lookout for new people. The Newcomers will throw two or three pool parties in the summer. There'll be a barbecue, volleyball, horseshoes. It tends to be an extraordinarily homogeneous group of people. The women talk about their cleaning ladies and their cars and how they're going to decorate their living room. The unifying factor for the men seems to be tennis, so they talk about tennis."

Dick jogs several miles every morning before going to work. He had recently been letting his hair grow, and the beginnings of a mustache were sprouting on his upper lip. People at work had been giving him flack about his hair.

"You've got to keep a tight rein on yourself out here," Dick remarked, "or you could fade away and never know the difference; just kiss off the next twenty years of your life. By then you'd have so many kids and you'd have become so soft that you'd be stuck for good."

It is the upper stratum that is responsible for Bedford's image to the rest of the world. A few representatives of the jet set number among their many residences around the world a retreat in Bedford. Once I whiled away a delightful afternoon in a poolhouse playing scrabble with a woman whose name apears frequently in the society columns. In the middle of the game she pushed a button under the table and suddenly every tree in sight was enveloped in a cloud of insecticide.

The most important element of prestige in Bedford, however, comes not from money or accomplishment, but from something called "background." There are those who have it and those who don't, and the world is divided, in the minds of those who feel they have it, along those lines.

One afternoon I called upon an extremely savvy and intelligent woman with an encyclopedic knowledge of Bedford society who has made the town her life study. Every morning she and her friends customarily log several hours on the phone, catching up on and disseminating "the latest," an activity which another member of the grapevine has called "beating the tom-tom." She knew what I was after, and having a sense of humor about her compulsion for being *au courant* she agreed to help me as long as she could remain anonymous. "I don't want publicity. I'm sixty-two and I want to be left alone. I don't mind having my name listed if I give ten dollars, but if I make a large contribution I want to be anonymous."

What, I began by asking her, is the significance of "background"? "There's an unconscious security that background gives you," she replied. "It's awkward to be confronted with a challenge to your background when it isn't there. After all, who are you? I haven't found it necessary to feature the fact that my ancestors came over on the *Mayflower,* or that they can be traced back to 1066." Then, pouring us a drink, she spoke a little about her involvements over the years—her dabbling in real estate and other "toys for a girl who wanted to be busy"; her lengthy stint in the Junior League, her membership in the District Nursing Association. "The snob appeal attracted support. It started out as a very precious little group. No question about it. Now it's more practical."

The conversation drifted to a comparison of Bedford with the other suburbs. "Scarsdale is high-powered competitive. Bedford is more comfortable. Why is a whole different culture represented in Scarsdale? They're doing it for show, and we want something quieter. This is a community that represents taste, taste in possessions, pride in the tiniest thing. I don't mean that they wear

Givenchy clothes. Do you want flash or fundamental quality? A lot of people around here could buy any car they want to. Just go down and write a check and drive it away. But instead they buy a Vega station wagon because it's functional and practical. They'd rather support other things. The kind of taste I'm talking about is not surface, it's basic."

Another tom-tom beater I interviewed a few days later echoed her sentiments; to this woman, Bedford represented "the essence of simplicity and dignity. The people don't want to put on a great show. They have shown great taste in being very simple, I think because of their background. I think Bedford has character. It has worn well. It has all been done in quite good taste and still we all had a lot of fun. But I don't know what's going to happen up here, because we're getting a lot of rich Jews. *I* have no objection to Jews as long as they keep quiet."

The style of Bedford is to play down one's wealth. In the heart of the old-line district, for example, is an enormous white-columned mansion, and painted on the mailbox that serves its occupants are the words "The Cottage." The roads in this section of Bedford are dirt, and riddled with potholes, washboards, and thankyou ma'ams that are ruinous to shock-absorbers. They're a problem to maintain but the residents feel so strongly about keeping them dirt that when, a few years ago, the town was planning to pave one of them, a group of prominent women lay down in front of the bulldozers and refused to get up until the machines had turned back and headed for the yard. The houses are often set back from the road and screened from view by dense tangles of vegetation. In their personal appearance the old guard of Bedford cultivates the English aristocratic look of studied seediness; the men putter about in old tweeds, the women garden in sensible shoes; returning home from Wall Street, the commuter slips out of his pin-striped suit and into his bib overalls. Worn-out loafers, not Guccis are the appropriate attire for the Club. In their sporting life the Bedford gentry also take after the English. At various times coaching and beagling have been popular, and currently some are going in for basseting.

It is considered an index of background, furthermore, to speak as if one were English, pronouncing the word "can't" to sound like the German philosopher, and the word "been" to sound like the leguminous vegetable. "All" is elongated to a majestic "awl," while "now" is clipped short to "na." "Bourbon on the rocks" comes out "böbon awn the rawks," with the lips hardly opened. Everything is uttered with a tone of blasé nasality, in the same tone of infinite boredom. It is interesting to hear women from the Midwest without background trying to get this accent down.

Social intercourse in the upper stratum calls for elaborate displays of politeness. People may despise each other, but they will never show it; it is almost as if the game is to be as *polite* to each other as possible. It is always "How nice to *see* you." In general, it is not "attractive" to show any emotions other than good cheer. Gatherings are by invitation only. The invitation to a cocktail party is likely to be written on heavy Tiffany stationery in a sprawling handwriting with a lot of curlicues and circles for dots perfected at an eastern boarding school.

After sex, the cocktail party is probably the most important cathartic and decongestant in exurbia. The man slips on his cranberry party pants, the woman tries to look as lush as possible, and it is an important release from the stresses and strains of fidelity, a break from what one man called his "mummified marriage" and an opportunity for a little harmless sexual flirtation. It is perfectly all right to put your hand on the bottom of someone else's wife at a cocktail party, as long as you don't keep it there long, or to kiss her quickly on the mouth; a certain amount of osculation is permissible. One old rogue is notorious for "Frenching" the young ladies. "He came up to me and kissed me, and suddenly I felt his tongue trying to get in," one of his victims told me with a shudder of disgust.

It's important to be mobile, to move deftly from one bunch of people to another. Casual groups of conversationalists are always forming, breaking up, and reforming, like clusters of grooming monkeys, and you have to be at liberty to flash quickly on someone or to linger and talk with them.

After a few drinks everybody feels looser and the noise level increases noticeably. In some of the people you sense a desperation behind the bubbling camaraderie. They're at the point where they've had a few scares, a disturbing EKG pattern, a marriage or two that didn't work out, a kid or two who didn't pan out, and they've learned to take it, to grin and bear it.

Cocktail parties will probably die out within the century. Nobody under thirty throws them. This realization imbues them with a special poignance for me. I always go when I'm invited. It never fails to be an educational experience. It's often the only way to find out what's happening.

You can tell a lot about communities from their country clubs. The Bedford Clubhouse is small and simple, and the atmosphere is relentlessly low-key. The red clay surface of the half-dozen tennis courts is excellent. Several times a day skeins of geese fly overhead, migrating from the water hazard on the tenth hole to various private ponds in the vicinity. Early on a Saturday morning several men in bright red or yellow slacks are already on the practice range, perfecting their drives. Here the upper class acquires its all-important proficiency in racket sports; the way you swing a racket is nearly as crucial an index of background as the way you speak. Only a few Jews have ever been admitted, and they are Jews who have assiduously assimilated the characteristics of the gentry. But even the fact that they belong represents a relaxation of the original policy. "Years ago," a member told me, "they wouldn't even let Benny Goodman play at six o'clock on Monday morning."

Several forces, both economic and social, now threaten the Club, and I doubt it will survive much longer than the cocktail party. The burgeoning tennis-bubble market and the many public courts that have sprung up in the area have made the game no longer the exclusive sport of the upper stratum. Money, particularly inherited money, is tighter these days, and some of the old families are discreetly resigning; so the Club is losing both its recreational value and its snob value.

The upper stratum itself is becoming, as one man put it, a "drying puddle." Part of the problem lies with the children. They just aren't coming back. Parent after parent has been disappointed by children who have rejected his cozy, undemocratic way of life. One father I know complained bitterly that his son had become "cynical, if not actually antagonistic, toward standards and ethics that I consider fundamental."

At the same time there are plenty of new aspirants who are dying to fill the vacant niches. People with new money, eager to acquire the proper trappings, are infiltrating the upper stratum as never before. The tom-tom beaters were extremely alarmed by this crass new element, this "profit without honor," as one of them put it, that is transmogrifying the scene. As a result the upper stratum is not the homogeneous WASP group it was even ten years ago.

William Cutler clears his throat and chuckles after almost everything he says. He seems to be very pleased with himself, and probably for good reason. He is an executive vice-president of a New York bank and a director of several companies. He is also a trustee of the Chapin School in the city and Rip out here, and is on the standing committee at Groton. Practically every Cutler in recent history has gone to Groton: His father, his two brothers, his son William III, and, now that Groton has become coeducational, his daughter Molly will be entering in the fall. "I was very careful not to push Groton, but they decided to go there anyway," he said, clearing his throat and chuckling.

"Bill III and Molly were accepted in all the wonderful halls of learning to which they had applied," his wife Jane told me. We were seated *en famille* in the living room. Jane was needlepointing the seat for a chair. Evidence of her creative talents abounded in the beautifully furnished house. A handsome colonial mantelpiece framed the fireplace. It had originally come from the drawing room of one Frederick R. Newbold and was described in a book Jane showed me called *Dutchess County Doorways and Other Examples of Period-Work in Wood:* "In its structural plan, border of dentil-pattern, and oval of gouged flutings it is typical of 1800."

Before coming to Bedford, the Cutlers lived in the city. "We rented up here twelve years ago, having summered the year before at Cold Spring Harbor," Jane said. "Long Island was so social you were in orbit every weekend. Out here you can call the shots. You don't *have* to see anyone. You can spend the whole weekend sitting by your pool if you want to."

"I know people around here whom I've known all my life and I only see them once a year at Caldor's," Bill said.

"We liked the people and we liked the smell of the hills," Jane went on, "so we moved out here. My better half drew up a list of requirements: beautiful view, away from highway, manageable house, privacy. We couldn't find a house. Then we saw this property, bought it and built this house.

"When I moved to the country I was used to doing a lot of things. I was very much involved in the Cosmopolitan Club and

147

the Philharmonic. Now I run a taxi service for my children, taking them to the Club, to Glasser's to buy their clothes for the fall, to the dentist and their friends' houses. At the moment we are getting ready for a month-long vacation in the Vineyard. I still go often to the Philharmonic and am on the parents' council at Rip and in the Bedford Garden Club. I am also a director of an organization devoted to preventing down-zoning and to maintaining the rural character of this lovely hamlet. I spend a lot of time on the phone arranging stupid meetings. Quite honestly, I'd like to have a regulated, self-contained job and not be fragmented like this."

"My weekends seem to go in all directions," Bill told me. "I cut down trees and split wood and catch up on the week's work, take care of the swimming pool, play some tennis but not so much as on the Vineyard or in the Caribbean. The children use the Club a lot but we only go two or three times a year."

"The wonderful thing about Bedford is that you can lead your own life," Jane said. "A lot of the snobbish aspects are dying out of themselves, and I don't think it's very nice to talk about them. And yet a lot of the differences are real, too. In the store I'm absolutely devoted to Mr. [a merchant], but if we ran into each other socially we'd talk for five minutes and then it would be rather sterile."

11 From Far Away
Across the Foam

The extent of the Italian presence in Westchester is not generally realized. But the truth is that Italian-Americans form the greatest segment of the population; that almost every artifact reflects, in some way, their shaping hand; that they dominate not only the construction industry, but most of the services, not to mention landscaping, catering, baking, hairdressing, law, politics, and practically everything else that makes the place run on a day-to-day basis.

In some parts of Westchester, where the *paesani* of an Italian village have relocated *en masse,* the fiesta of its patron saint is still celebrated. Elmsford has a feast of Our Lady of Mount Carmel, Port Chester honors St. Anthony of Padua, and in Verplanck there is a big feast of the Madonna. The town of Cortlandt, which includes Croton, Oscawana, Verplanck, and several other Hudson River villages, has the most closely knit Italian-American communities in the county. Mamaroneck is about sixty-percent Italian. On Main Street, the movie house shows pictures in the mother tongue.

The first wave came in 1880, the year there were twelve thousand Italian immigrants. Before long, the figure rose as high as three hundred thousand a year. Four-fifths of them were from Sicily and the lower part of the boot, where the soil, denuded of trees since Roman times, had long been exhausted. The social structure offered those at the bottom of it little more than a life of unremitting toil and misery. Children were put to work early and were often adept at several trades before they were fifteen.

During the 1880s a series of record-breaking droughts plagued southern Italy. In 1887 an epidemic of cholera broke out. Shortly afterward an economic crisis was precipitated by France's imposition of a high tariff on Italian wines. The economy went into deeper decline as Italy lost the major importer of her lemons and oranges—the United States, which was developing its own citrus-fruit industry. In 1906 Vesuvius erupted, leaving thousands homeless. Then in 1914 a world war broke out. Each of these calamities sent a wave of Italians over to America. To date five million souls have resettled here—a number surpassed only by the Germans.

Many of these new arrivals were drawn to Westchester, where a variety of menial jobs beckoned. The New York reservoir system was being laid out and there were dams to build and bridges, pipelines, viaducts, aqueducts, and traction systems; and low-lying hamlets like Katonah to move to higher ground. The railroad was extending its track north up the Harlem valley from Mount Kisco, and there were roads to build, power, telephone, and telegraph wires to string, stone and sand to quarry, houses to put up, and walls to stack. This was the kind of work the Italian laborer was used to doing, and he became a ditch-digger, a hod-carrier, mortar-mixer, or sandhog, believing that if he worked hard and saved up, he could set himself up in a business of his own in a few years, go back to Italy and find a wife, or bring over the one he'd left behind.

The great achievement of Italian manual labor in Westchester is the New Croton Dam in Ossining. It was started in 1892 and was regarded at the time of its completion in 1907 as "the eighth wonder of the world." By any standards it is an impressive structure: The huge blocks of gabbro, white granite, and marble, taken from a quarry a mile and a quarter away, rise in a tapering curve to a height of two hundred and ninety feet on a foundation sunk a hundred and twenty-four feet below the river bed. A decorative corniced border runs along the top layer of blocks between two of the three buttresses and under the concrete road where motorists can get out, lean on the silver-painted guard rail, and take in the view. The great dam spans twenty-six hundred feet in all, looming over the Croton Gorge and a small county park with scattered maples and evergreens far below. It holds back thirty-two billion gallons, whose overflow, released gradually over a series of steps into a thousand-foot long spillway, runs under a huge steel arch and then comes thundering down into the gorge in three stages, with natural outcroppings of rock to break its fall, throwing up mist, rainbows, and a fresh organic smell. Some courageous graffitist must have lowered himself down on a rope to paint, on a rock face right above the cascades, the words ERICA '75, and someone else, a little farther up, SQUIT '73.

The people who built the dam lived at its foot and in the surrounding hills, in colonies with boarding houses, saloons, shops, and chapels. Mostly single men, they played cards, *bocce*, *amura* (two or more people shooting out their fingers and betting on the outcome). The well-to-do would titillate themselves by driving through the Italian ghettos and labor camps that had cropped up around the county. Unsolved thefts and rapes were commonly pinned on "those greasy Italians," and some up-county communities were in such mortal fear of them that they deed-restricted against Italians until only a few years ago.

One of the seamier Italian ghettos was Sutton's Row in Mount Kisco. It had no toilets or running water and harbored gangsters. Three-fingered Brown and John Dillinger both hid out in cellars on Sutton's Row for a while. But it was also the home of hard-working artisans—bricklayers, masons, plasterers, cabinetmakers, and the like; the *mastris* or tradesmen.

There were two periods of wall-building in Westchester, quite recognizable from each other although both used the same medium—the gneisses and schists of the county's bedrock. The earlier walls were laid by settlers who were mainly concerned with getting the boulders out of the way, dragging them to the edge of the fields with horse- or ox-drawn stoneboats, and stacking them up into walls that would serve as boundary lines and fences for livestock. Every winter the frost would heave up a new "stone crop," to be gathered and added to the walls. You find these crude walls and piles of small rocks, all over the woods. They serve little purpose now except as to give shelter to squirrels, chipmunks,

151

shrews, spiders, lichens, and a host of other woodland organisms, and to prevent windthrown poles of timber from total prostration. Between natural weathering, slap-dash construction, and people raiding them there isn't much left of these walls, some of which date back to the late seventeenth century. Occasionally, though, some care was put into them: There's a showcase dry wall near the superintendent's office at the Pound Ridge Reservation, for example, that was laid well over a hundred years ago and so perfectly that a full-grown man can still run along the flat slabs on top and jump up and down on them to his heart's delight, and none of them will rock.

The second period of stonework lasted from about 1880 to 1930. These walls are mostly to be found on the estates and along the roads, and they were laid by Italian masons in whose blood the stacking of rock from the arid slopes of the Appenines into walls and dwellings had been running for centuries. Most of the walls are wet, but the dry ones are still largely intact, too, and display the highest craftsmanship. While the walls remain, however, stonemasonry is a lost trade, and only a few old-timers are still around who know how to do it. One of the last and greatest of Westchester's wallmen was the legendary Vincenzo Ingegneri, a Sicilian who kept working until his death a few years ago at the age of eighty-two. People who knew him described him as "slender and not particularly robust-looking," but he "would swing large boulders into place with a few apparently effortless tilts and twists." One of his employers explained his *modus operandi*: "I asked him 'do you want anybody to work with you, Mr. Ingegneri?' 'Just my plank and crowbar.' Sometimes his grandsons would help him. First he'd dig a ditch three feet deep. Then he wanted big stones. Then he'd ask for head-size stones or fist-size stones. He would break them with one blow of the hammer." When bad weather kept Vincenzo home, he would pace the family living room "as if he were in a cage."

I was sitting in Leonardi's, having a slice and a Bud and reading a magazine while my laundry was drying next door. Leonardi's is a small pizzeria that occupies a thirteen-foot-wide strip between the Village Launder-Aid and Luppino's deli opposite Leonard Park in Mount Kisco (hence its name). I had just noticed the simulated insect holes in the simulated wood panels with which the room is sided and was thinking about what a nice touch when the waitress placed a dessert plate on my table and said, "The boss wants you to try his mother's macaroni cake." It was delicious. I looked into the kitchen and thanked Ralph Esposito, the short, stone-faced boss. "Come back after twelve o'clock Holy Saturday," he said. "We're gonna have something special." Italian Catholics, I learned two days later, abstain from meat on Good Friday till noon on the following day. They traditionally break their fast with *pizza rustica*, a thick, quichelike dish consisting of goat's cheese (*farmagette*), home-made hard salami, hard-boiled eggs, and *mozzarella*. It has no tomatoes, which are an American additive.

"Leonardi's is a family business," he explained. His father-in-law, Eugenio Gaudio, is "my ambassador at the table. He keeps everybody happy. Talks about the old bootleg days." His father, Raphael, is the "official sauce-maker," while his mother, Angelina, keeps "behind the scenes, makes soup and all the goodies at home." His wife, Gloria, "takes care of the finances and makes the best cheesecake ever invented." Two of his daughters, Christine and Gina, help out at the tables, while the youngest, Nancy, is just starting.

Another key figure in the operation and an honorary member of the Esposito family is Anthony Costa. Tony came from Portugal in 1962. He has twinkling blue eyes, long, strong forearms, and a good word for everybody who comes in. He can usually be found standing on a platform that was built especially for him (both he and Ralph are five feet even) stretching doughballs out on a marble slab that came from Italy. Behind him is a poster of a blonde bombshell who is saying, "My thoughts are with you, Mr. Pizzaman." It is educational to watch him knead the dough with his fists and toss it up in the air and spin it around with both hands until it lands back on the slab perfectly round and flat and ready to be smothered with ingredients. Spinning dough requires the agility of a juggler.

It was Tony who tipped me off about Carmen Carrozza, the foremost accordionist in Westchester County. The great Carrozza lives on a quiet street in Thornwood. He was born in Calabria in 1924 and came to Chappaqua in 1930. The street he grew up on was totally Calabrian. At an early age Carmen showed a definite inclination toward music. He never seemed to tire of hearing his father play the two or three songs he knew on "the old squeezebox," the semi-tone accordion. When the boy was eight, his father sent him to a music school down the street, where he took up the violin. This led to accordion lessions in New York, apprenticeship with Hugo Giganti, the reigning accordionist of his day, and, finally, a concert debut in Philadelphia in 1947. Since then he has performed in Boston with the Pops and several times in Carnegie Hall. In 1957 he opened a music school, which offers instruction in piano, drums, guitar, and organ, as well as accordion. There are few Italians in Westchester who haven't heard of the great Carrozza. Italians hold artists in the same esteem as doctors and professors. "To us the doors have always been open and more than that. Once you said Carrozza you were treated royally. But it hasn't been so easy for most Italians. They never had the in. Like a guy wanted to be a cop, there was nobody there to help him, or he wanted to be a doctor, the college would make it hard for him. It's still hard in some professions. Today you got a lot of Italians in construction, landscaping, and the third genera-tion since the turn of the century has started being lawyers and being able to get into politics. And of course music—trumpets, marching bands, club dates—all-around musicians—there's a lot of Italians in it yet.

"Italians do what comes naturally. If they like music, even if they don't think there's much money in it, they'll go into it anyway. They're an expressive people, and music being a traditional expressive artistic form it hits home. Of course they're very romantic and sensitive, the Italians, too."

No tale of the Italian presence would be complete without mention of the Mafia. "You only hear about it when something bad happens," one Italian told me. "As soon as someone is killed they say, 'It looks like a Mafia job.' But it's really like a close brotherhood. If something happens to a family like sickness or death they're known to help them out of it. The word Mafia means a 'sophisticate.' There are nightclubs and bars all over Italy called 'Il Mafioso' and so forth which have nothing to do with any criminal activity. On top of the list with the Mafia is trusting each other. If you double-cross them, you had better watch it. But as long as you hold your word, they can be good people to deal with."

Westchester County District Attorney Carl A. Vergari was less charitable about the "Robin Hood mythology" that surrounds the *cosa nostra*. "That's garbage," he pronounced emphatically from behind his desk in the County Center in White Plains. "All they are is punks, gangsters, hoodlums who have these units called families with an infrastructure. At the same time, it's unfair that organized crime is presented as an Italian venture. Within the structure of the underworld there *is* a group that is Italian, but they are connected to a larger network that reaches across the country. This group is an important part of the total organized crime picture in the U.S., but an infinitesimal part of the Italians in Westchester County."

An imposing and well-spoken figure who was wearing a black pin-striped suit, Vergari himself represented an interesting phenomenon—that of the Italians who have entered public office within the last ten years and come to dominate Westchester politics. At present we have not only Vergari as our district attorney but a county supervisor by the name of Alfred del Bello, while the supervisor of the town of Bedford is a man named Albert Marchigianni. It is not really surprising that a large percentage of the elected officials in the county is of Italian descent because the Italian vote is estimated to be between forty and forty-five percent. Once elected, the Italian politician tends to prove very able, because of his pragmatic, down-to-earth temperament. "We are a practical-minded people," Vergari explained, "and will try to make use of opportunities as we see them. We don't waste time over what we can't have. You've heard the expression, 'An honest day's work for an honest day's pay.' Well, that's the way we operate."

According to Vergari, the two main operations in which organized crime has a hand in Westchester are gambling and loan-sharking. "Millions of Westchester dollars are involved in the numbers racket, in bookmaking and sports betting." I told him that I'd been eating a hot dog in front of a certain lunch-wagon the other day, and a man had pulled up in a sausage truck with New Jersey plates and placed a twenty-dollar bet with the owner of the wagon on the outcome of a horse race to be run that afternoon. "He may have been an independent," Vergari said, "but chances are he was a 'writer' who turns his sheet over to somebody else. As a 'writer' he gets twenty-five percent right off the top. The next level, the first executive, is the 'comptroller.' He can have forty-fifty writers who turn in to him. He usually has a 'pick-up man,' a paid employee who picks up for him. The betting deadline is not much later than twelve noon. The comptroller gets ten percent and is usually a salaried member in a 'bank' where the bets are reviewed. Four to eight comptrollers belong to a bank. The money is kept separate from the slips because it is forfeitable in a bust. We busted a big bank in Eastchester six or seven years ago in a building which had formerly housed the Chamber of Commerce. The seal was still on the front door. The comptrollers would get there after midnight and work through dawn getting ready for the day's action. Subsequently, we broke up several other banks, and after that they moved out of the county. Recently, in conjunction with the State Police, we busted a big bank across the river in Rockland County.

"But as for the man on the street placing a bet with a bookie, there's no way in the world we can stop it. We don't even try here. The local police departments are in charge of that."

I mentioned a recent multi-million-dollar drug ring which had been broken by the Bedford police. Before closing in on the house where the dope was being kept a plainclothes detective had spent several months observing it while pretending to fish in a nearby lake. On the night of the raid everyone in the ring had left the house, but the police confiscated some barrels in the cellar which contained several tons of marijuana. All the parties were eventually apprehended, and the papers reported that the operation had an "alleged Mafia connection." I asked Vergari about the case.

"Drugs?" he said. "I don't waste my time wondering if it's Mafia. They're not a big force in drugs. The top-level Mafia has long since ceased to be an active force in narcotics except as financiers. A man might come to them and say, 'I have a chance to bring in a ship. It'll cost a hundred grand but I can get six hundred grand in two weeks.' So the guy will lend him the money at two and a half percent a week. But it's very hard to finger a loan shark. You have to prove that he knew what the money was going for. Most of the loan-sharking is with legitimate business people whose credit has gone dry. It's risky: if you can't pay it back." I drew my first finger horizontally across my throat and looked at Vergari questioningly. He nodded.

The private carting business in Westchester is also widely thought to be controlled by criminal elements. In 1974 the *New York Times* ran a story about the A-1 Compaction Corporation, founded by Nicholas Rattenni, who has been identified on the charts of the Senate investigations as a *soldato* or soldier, in the Vito Genovese family and the reputed head of the Genovese carting operations in the county. Rattenni's adopted son, Alfred, runs the business now, and it's been under intensive investigation, but so far the District Attorney's office has been unable to find any evidence of wrongdoing. Rattenni had bought up a number of small garbage removal services, none of whom, however, would admit that they had been forced to sell out. They claimed to have been offered a good price.

In recent years, Vergari explained, the tendency has been for the second generation, the sons of known underworld figures, to go into legitimate businesses—restaurants, apartment houses, clubs, and the like. So-called Mafia-operated night clubs have the reputation for being extremely well run. "Here again," Vergari said, "there's been no evidence of wrongdoing where you could put anybody in jail. Maybe it's unfair to 'visit the sins of the father.' Most of the time they go into the businesses for legitimate investment purposes but sometimes they do it to milk the business for what it's worth, then destroy it—the old bankruptcy caper— leave your creditors holding the bag. But that, too, is hard to prove."

A final possible area of Mafia involvement is the construction industry. "There are a lot of Italians in this business," Vergari said, "coming from a heritage of artisans and engineers and manual labor. And of course when a contract is awarded by such and such a town, more suspicion will attach to an Italian company than it would to, say, an Irish one. There are always rumors that in obtaining such and such a contract improper influences were used . . ."

To get both sides of the story I needed to find someone actually connected with the Mafia who would be willing to talk under the promise of complete anonymity. After discreetly letting the word be passed in the Italian community about what I was after, someone finally gave me a name. "He could maybe tell you something about it, but don't tell him I sent you," my source pleaded.

I found the man who was supposed to know something about the Mafia standing in his driveway with a saw in one hand, looking at the trees along it which he had just pruned. He was an old man, close to eighty, and from a distance he seemed like a typical Italian laborer in his drab gray jacket and pants and brown cap. Gently placing his hand on my shoulder, he suggested that we sit in the sun-deck chairs in his backyard. It was a perfect day for sitting out in the sun. The shadows of the late afternoon sun were streaming over the lawn, and besides, he said, his wife didn't feel too well and was sleeping in the house.

We began by talking about "old times." He told me how he'd come from Calabria when he was sixteen, how he'd got his first job spading up a piece of ground on an estate where they were going to put in pumpkins. "The Italians were a hard-working people," he said. "They came over with nothing, and now everybody has their own homes." He himself had been living in this house for forty-six years. Friends in the different trades—plumbers, carpenters, masons—had let him have their work on time, and he'd paid them back slowly and in different ways, almost losing the house once to a creditor who had at the last moment committed suicide. He'd risen in one of the labor unions to become a "business representative." "My job was to see that everybody got paid." He'd retired after fifty-seven years in the union, and now he had his four acres to keep up, and grandsons.

I asked him what he knew about the Mafia and he did a slight take, then said, "I never heard of the Mafia. I don't even own a gun. I got this woodchuck who comes into my garden. I'd like to get him but I don't even know how to shoot." I told him I had heard plenty of stories about so-called Mafia rubouts and gangland slayings and that wasn't what I was interested in. I wanted to hear the good side, if there was one; what the *cosa nostra* stood for, and what its members believed in. Hadn't it begun as a sort of brotherhood? The old man thought for a while and after again denying that he knew anything about the Mafia he said, "The Mafia is like the Elks Club. You got to go through an examination to get in. It's no different from any other segment, just using muscle to get your way, to tell your enemies you're equal.

"I tell you a story. A big man and a little man were working together, building a well on the big man's property. And the big man got mad at the little man and punched him in the face until his nose started to bleed. Then the little man went home and as he stood at the sink washing his nose he thought of how he could get even. Then he went to his neighbor and said you know a woodchuck has been getting into my garden and eating my tomatoes and squash. Let me have your gun so I can shoot it. So the little man took his neighbor's gun and went to another friend and said I'm going to shoot this woodchuck but what am I going to skin it with? Can you lend me your knife? So the little man took his friend's knife—it was about this long [shows]—and sticks it into his belt. Then he goes back to the big man's house. The big man sees him coming with a gun and a knife and starts to run but the little man says, very calmly, stay where you are, because if you try to run, I'll shoot you. And he walked up to the big man and said, look, my nose is still bleeding, and the big man pleaded with him, please forgive me. I forgive you, the little man said. I'm not going to shoot. And then he took the knife out of his belt and stuck it between the big man's ribs. I'm going to stab you. No. I'm going to throw you into the well. See? Shoot him, stab him, or drown him, that man's going to die any way you look at it. You call that Mafia? That's just human nature. The little fellow has to find ways and means of getting even."

When he had finished the old man looked at me and gave me a brilliant warm smile that was like the kiss of death.

Edward Scardaccione is to my knowledge the oldest person in Westchester. I was going up the stairs of the Mount Kisco Medical Group one afternoon to see my doctor when I found my way blocked by an old man who was being helped up the stairs by another man and a woman. "Careful. He's a hundred and four," the woman told me proudly. There was nothing wrong with Scardaccione. He was just having a check-up. Born in Naples, he had landed in New York in 1902, worked for sixty years as a mechanical engineer, and had been making the rounds of his children ever since. I asked his son-in-law, Samuel Schecter, the secret of his longevity, and since he was a retired doctor, Schecter was able to give me a rather complete answer. "Things don't bother him," he said. "The fact that he's able to throw things off easily is probably the main factor. He can get into a violent argument one minute and be perfectly calm the next. He expresses his emotions and doesn't keep them in where they can eat away at you. His blood pressure's normal. 'Old age' is his only health problem. His main form of exercise is indoor discussion."

12 The Lower Tier

There is a distinctly European aspect to White Plains. The architecture, a mixture of staid Tudor apartment buildings, large department stores, and rundown rowhouses could be that of Birmingham, Le Havre, or some other provincial capital. The vegetation, planted deliberately or escaped, is mostly European. London planes, copper beeches, Norway maples, and ginkgos, capable of withstanding the fumes, line the boulevards. The senior citizens who sit on the public benches, gather wild onion and dandelion greens along the river parkways, and search the last shreds of woods for mushrooms are European—Eastern European for the most part—with little English.

How White Plains got its name is not immediately apparent. I stopped a number of inhabitants on the streets and asked them what the name alluded to but none could come up with the answer. Earlier in the century a man named John Rosch made it his business to find out just how White Plains did get its name and his monograph, which appeared in 1939, is still the definitive treatment of the subject. "I think the first settlers were not wholly felicitous in christening their hamlet," Rosch conceded. "The prevalence of white balsam shrubs hereabouts" was offered by one source which Rosch dug up as a possible solution, but I had a lot of trouble running down what white balsam shrubs were: whether they were in fact saplings of a kind of poplar known as tacamahac or balm of Gilead or not shrubs at all, but an everlasting herb in the composite family called sweet white balsam and more commonly referred to as cat's-foot. Having seen the silver undersides of the leaves in a vast stand of poplar fluttering up in the breeze, and hillsides in the summer smothered with hoary influorescences of pearly everlasting like a blanket of frost, I can visualize either explanation. Now that most of White Plains is tarred over we'll never know.

Apparently Mr. Rosch was not aware that the Algonquian name for the area was *Qua-rop-pas,* a word meaning "White marshes." By the late nineteenth century the meadows and pastures around White Plains were reportedly filled with daisies until they looked snow-covered even in the month of June. But there were no daisies, which are alien, in Westchester at the time the deed was purchased from the Indians in 1683. Maybe the explanation is that when the Indians first got there, there was a lot of snow on the ground. Or maybe there was an outcrop of some pale mineral like the chalk that gave rise to the White Cliffs of Dover. Rosch's own personal theory had to do with a low-lying fog. "I've seen mist and fog rising from the swamplands in enveloping clouds that remained suspended in midair for days at a time," he argued persuasively. It's possible, but there are not enough undeveloped swamps around any more to verify it, and no gases now except those emitted by cars and factory smokestacks.

The Plains may have been white once, but the only word for them now is gray. It is the pervasive, grubby grayness that lies like a film over the entire lower county, so palpable that the old people on the public benches customarily sit on sections of the *Daily News,* and the proper black man at the bus stop wedges the *Reporter Dispatch* between his elbow and the greasy cement wall against which he is leaning. In this part of Westchester a black race of gray squirrels starts to appear in north White Plains, becoming more abundant farther south. Their unusual pigmentation may be an adaptive response like the "industrial melanism" that caused white moths to become black during the Industrial Revolution in the nineteenth-century England, when the bark of the trees they rested on was darkened by soot. Many gray squirrels in the north-county have chestnut ridges along the tail which continue up the spine, but none are soot-colored. Air pollution in lower Westchester has certainly had an effect on other indigenous organisms. Below White Plains certain lichens that are susceptible to it do not grow.

The last time I was in White Plains it was Christmastime. Santa Claus in effigy was everywhere. I was with a friend who had just come from California with her four-year-old daughter. She noticed two things: the superabundance of travel agencies and the pallid faces of the people rushing past a Salvation Army soldier with his hand-bell and contribution pot. Slick chicks, black and white, in buffalo sandals, bandanas, and the latest styles hurried in and out of the department stores. White Plains is the place where career-minded Westchester girls flock. The tallest buildings between New York and Albany are in White Plains. No other city its size in America—fifty thousand, quadrupling on a work day—boasts so many prestigious retail stores: B. Altman, Bergdorf Goodman, Saks, Sears, Alexander's, Wallach's, Goldsmith Brothers, Brentano's, Black, Starr, and Frost, Jaeger International, Bloomingdale's, and Abraham and Straus. In all, over a thousand retail outlets generated $280 million in volume for White Plains in 1974. The only comparable volume is in Stamford, Connecticut, another satellite city of New York. Even more important than being the county seat, White Plains is the shopping capital of Westchester. It sets the tone for smaller, ambitious centers like Mount Kisco. Members of the Mount Kisco Chamber of Commerce dream of having big-name department stores and four-story municipal parking garages like those in White Plains.

We went into Sears to hunt down Santa Claus for little Tessa. He was not among the freezers, washers, refrigerators, lawnmowers, robes and loungewear, men's furnishings, or luggage. Sears does not have a Santa Claus. "He's at Macy's," a helpful salesgirl told us.

Macy's was a bit more refined than Sears, but not as refined as Lord and Taylor. The salesgirls were young, svelte, spiffy, and toothsome. Everywhere on the selling floor people were handling, touching, feeling. We found Santa sitting on a golden throne on the third floor and making himself accessible to children. He was attended by a photographer. You could have a picture taken of yourself sitting on Santa's lap.

"What's your favorite thing to do in the winter?"

"Ice-skating."

"Thanks for coming to see me."

The man behind the big white beard was a twenty-two-year-old professional actor. He had been on and off Broadway, and was currently experiencing the first slump of his career. He had started the day after Thanksgiving and would be playing Santa until Christmas Eve. After this gig he didn't know what would happen. "Maybe I'll go over to Bamberger's and play the Easter bunny," he joked.

"It's pure joy by far," he continued. "Kids feel a great responsibility to Santa Claus and you have to meet that yourself. That's why I go to these lengths to put on makeup, rouge, and clown white on the brows and under the eyes. I use basic clown makeup because when you think about it Santa's a clown." After Tessa had gone up to him blushing all over, whispered into his ear what she wanted, and run back to her mother, he went on. "It's real. I think it's a good fantasy. I did a lot of thinking about it and I couldn't think of any time the Santa Claus myth had ever hurt anybody. You put on this suit and this stuff and it gives you license to be crazy and I like that an awful lot.

"I start out with basics like name and age and school and they usually take it from there. I just try to pick up on their energy. They ask you the questions about your reindeer and things. I'm not a boisterous Santa Claus, I'm not a ho-hoer, cause I think it's an intimate moment. It's pure magic." Waiting shyly in the wings was a little black boy who had never met Santa before, and Santa beckoned to him, giving me a final aside: "I think I'm an unusual department-store Santa Claus."

Life Savers are, of course, "the candy with a hole." They are essentially liquid sugar and corn syrup cooked under a vacuum till they become a plastic mass you could pick up with gloves if you wanted to. The plastic mass is dumped into a tray where colors and flavors are kneaded in by machine. Then another machine called the "spinner" rolls the mass into a rope and feeds it into a third machine that stamps out the candy at the rate of four thousand per minute. Then it's cooled and packaged.

All this takes place at the Life Saver plant in Port Chester, a fine, old five-story factory with a green tile roof and concrete Life Savers under the windows. Life Savers were invented in Cleveland, briefly manufactured in Brooklyn, and have been turned out here exclusively since 1919. Along one side of the building there are three monumental rolls of Life Savers—pep-o-mint, orange, and wint-o-green—and along another there are two more, wild cherry and assorted flavors. Mounted horizontally on poles, the rolls are about ten feet long and open at one end, from which the candy dangles enticingly in thin air. A strong confectionery odor floats down from the plant and percolates through the grimy brick facades along the old main street of Port Chester. Port Chester looks no different from a hundred other decaying northeastern factory towns. Life Saver, Inc., is about the last major industry here, outside of Marvel Mystery Oil, a gas additive whose headquarters are across the street. The R.B.W. Bolt Factory used to be in Port Chester, but it went down south a couple of years ago. Of course, down in Mamaroneck the Herb-Ox people are still putting out their redoubtable bouillon cubes.

My contact with the Life Saver plant was Danny Delaney, who two years ago was one of their chewing-gum tasters. His actual job was a little more complicated than just tasting chewing gum, I discovered. First he had to make it. Officially Danny was a technician in the Research and Development prototype lab, a futuristic and practically windowless building next to the old plant. Strangers weren't allowed to witness the actual making of the candy, not only because of Food and Drug health regulations, but because the process itself is very hush-hush. Security in the Life Saver plant is strict. A man in a blue uniform sits at the door checking passes. The public has to content itself with a display window showing the thirty-two flavors of Life Savers that are made within the bowels of the plant.

As I walked past the plant on the way to see Danny, a man who was making inflammatory-sounding remarks in Spanish handed me a blue leaflet from Local 50 Bakery and Confectionery Workers Union. It said, among other things: "Siempre hay *ALGUNOS*, que *VENDAN A SUS COMPAÑEROS DE TRABAJO* y *LOS TIREN AL RIO PAR DOS DOZENAS DE HUEVOS* y *UNA LIBRA DE MANTEQUILLA*."

Another man handed me a yellow sheet which said the same thing in English: "There are always a *FEW* who will *sell their co-workers DOWN THE RIVER* for the price of *TWO (2) DOZEN EGGS & A POUND OF BUTTER*."

Then it went on to tell the story of one AVA FULCHER who

had been employed as a general helper on March 15 and fired two (2) days later. Her supervisor had told her that she had too many *BAD LOLLIPOPS* and also that she was *YAWNING* on the job.

"*SO BEWARE* [the leaflet concluded]—*DON'T YAWN ON THE JOB.*"

Things in Research and Development were a little looser. "Nobody's on your back," Danny said to me as we stood in a roomful of desks separated by pegboard dividers. "It goes in cycles. Sometimes we work really hard to get something out, other times we slack off. Today is kind of slow." A medley of Muzak, including the theme from *Mary Hartman, Mary Hartman* and the Beatles was being piped in through hidden speakers. No one else was in the room.

"A lot I can't talk about, especially recipes and ingredients," he went on, leading me into the lab. The Prototype Department was made up of three people. There was "the creative guy." His job was "to get products that are not out there—say a noncariogenic (non-decay-producing) Life Saver, or a new antacid or breath mint.

The supervisor tries to figure out how to make the creative guy's new ideas into a viable product. He translates the ideas into formulae which he gives to the technician, who makes them up into actual samples. Near Danny's desk was a brown bottle with a label that said AROMALOK SWEET BIRCH SOUTHERN TYPE 180779. It contained sweet oil of birch, the essential oil of several plants—black birch, winterberry, and teaberry. The oil had been spray-dried into a powder and was almost pure methyl silicilate, the main flavor of wint-o-green Life Savers. Danny had recently used it in the preparation of a prototype breath mint that he was not at liberty to discuss.

Danny spent a lot of time in the four environmental rooms where, his supervisor explained, "we accelerate aging. Is it going to oxidize? Is the flavor going to leach out of the package? We want to know what the product will be like after it's been sitting on the shelf two years. Obviously we can't leave it on the shelf for that long because time is at a premium." A week in the environmental room, he explained, was the equivalent of a month on the shelf.

Once a promising prototype has been made up, it goes to Quality Control, a department in the old plant, where it is tested by a panel of twenty or thirty tasters. If they like it, it is given a

166

consumer test. "Give it to the people," the creative guy explained, "and say, here is the product. Eat it, taste it. Test the functionability of it. Then give it a market test. Set up one-third of the country.

"The greatest consumer of Life Savers and chewing gum is the teenager," he went on. "It's a tremendous business. Fantastic amounts of money to play around with."

The Lower Tier is made up of the southernmost communities, which either border the Bronx—Yonkers, Mount Vernon, and Pelham—or Long Island Sound—New Rochelle, Larchmont, Mamaroneck, Rye, and Port Chester. White Plains is also considered by some to be in the Lower Tier. Seventy percent of Westchester's people live here on thirty percent of the land. Much of it is rubble. Urban decay rages unchecked in some of the communities. Municipalities sprawl into each other, losing their integrity. You can't tell, for example, where Mount Vernon ends and Yonkers begins. There are few green spaces, mostly along the Hutchinson, Bronx, and Saw Mill River parkways. Most of Westchester's blacks and Hispanics live in the Lower Tier.

It is hard to feel a sense of continuity in the Lower Tier since most of the landscape has been built over three or four times. It is hard to visualize that the immense Cross-County Shopping Center, for instance, was once deep woods, or that there used to be secret lakes only a few neighborhood kids knew about in Eastchester. I made a special trip to Otsego County to talk with Ed Urich who grew up in Mount Vernon, left in the thirties, and hasn't been back since. I thought his perspective on the Lower Tier would be interesting, and it was. The world he remembered was small enough that a person could know it well. Now it's so vast and sprawling that it's unknowable. "Down in New Rochelle there was a squab farm," he recalled as we sat at his modest kitchen table. "The bootlegger was in White Plains. The Boston and Westchester Railroad ran an electric line from 133rd Street in the Bronx as far as Westchester Avenue in Port Chester, then ran out of money. As kids we used to find Spanish doubloons in Wolf Lane in Pelham Manor. Hartsdale was where they had the animal cemetery. A lot of famous people had their pets buried there. It even had an elephant. There was a famous murder in Hartsdale. They cut up the body of a gal by the name of Peacock and threw it into the quarry. And of course you know Hollywood started in New Rochelle. It was one of the first places they made animated cartoons—*Terry Tunes*—and Pathé newsreels. Norman Rockwell lived there for a while. And who was it always sang the "Star-Spangled Banner"? She was a fat little opera singer. She lived on East Lincoln Avenue in Mount Vernon and was in the San Francisco earthquake. I remember her telling me that. Mabel something.

"After World War I the high-school girls became emancipated and started to raise hell. They made up dances like the bunny hop, the black bottom, and the big apple. They formed a club called Our Mother's Little Lambs and it ended up with twelve of the boys and girls drowning stark naked in a Model T that fell through the ice of Lake Siwanoy in Eastchester. They left one girl naked on a buoy in Larchmont Harbor and she was supposed to swim a mile and a half to shore as her initiation. I picked her up in my boat and took her to the yacht club."

Urich pulled out of Mount Vermin, as he calls it, in 1938. "I just got fed up with it down there. I just wanted to get out in the country and Otsego County is where my mother's folks came from. I don't want to go back either. From what I hear they've blown it."

One place that's still there from Urich's day is the Sacred Heart Monastery, which gives its name to the Monastery section of North Yonkers. "Every kid in the southern part of the county called it the Pope Manufacturing Company," he told me. I'd always admired the view of the Monastery section from the Saw Mill River Parkway, particularly at night: ten thousand lighted windows on the hillsides; thin slits shimmering from the people's closely packed houses below them, in the valley; the black stacks of the city incinerator and the factories—Anaconda Cable, Precision Valve, Aerosol Spray Can, Otis Elevator, Yonkers Granite-Tombstone; dominating the hilltop, the red brick belltower of the monastery, and in the distance, through a gap in the ridge, the dark basaltic columns of the New Jersey Palisades on the other side of the Hudson.

For years I knew it only that way, as a distant tableau. Then, one cold Sunday, I decided to enter it. I got off at the Tuckahoe exit of the Saw Mill, drove down Stratton Street past an eye bank, and parked. The rest of the street consisted of a group of detached houses of varying vintage. Some of them were still bordered with multicolored blinking bulbs although it was already February. Behind the houses were garden plots, goat-sheds, and grape arbors. Halfway down the street I came upon a man standing in front of a partly constructed frosted brick house with a brown-shingled mansard roof, not unlike the roof on a McDonald's restaurant. He was short, stocky, and wore a three-piece beige suit woven in a pattern that was hard to look at for very long. His hands were in his pockets, jingling keys or change, and he was whistling briskly. He had a big broad chest that stuck out, as if expecting medals, and his thick accent was Slavic.

The hill we were on, he explained, was known as Bryn Mawr. It was a Slavic neighborhood—Polish, Russian, Rumanian, Hungarian, with some Greeks. Monastery, across the valley, was Irish working class all the way up the hill but on top, by the monastery itself, in a section called Park Hill, it was well-to-do Italians—doctors, lawyers, white-collar professionals.

I went down into the valley and stopped at a stucco Alamo-type pizzeria called the Capri, where I had calzoni. Two boys on skateboards were slaloming down the steeply graded sidewalk, maneuvering deftly through a course of parking meters. A number of unusually fine-looking teenage girls walked by. Yonkers has produced more Miss New Yorks than any other municipality in the state.

I reached the monastery in time for five o'clock mass. All over the hill people were streaming out of houses in their Sunday best, walking through yards that had Madonna shrines and lines of laundry, and heading toward the sound of the bells. Once inside the church they would dip their fingers in holy water, walk up to the altar, drop to one knee, and cross themselves. I went up to a man who stood at the head of the center aisle clasping a black rosary.

"You a member of this church?" I asked him.

"Yeah. You wanna buy it?" he answered, looking at me through sad, kind, watery bloodshot eyes. He was an usher. I told him I just wanted to look around. He handed me a program and recommended the view from the balcony.

Upstairs a handsome young man with a brown mustache and a plaid scarf wrapped around his neck was seating himself at the organ. After adjusting his shirtsleeves he picked up a phone that was connected to the side of his instrument and told someone on the other end that he was ready. Then he pressed his fingers down on the keyboard and the vaulted ceilings of the church began to resound with the strains of Handel's *Hallelujah* chorus.

In the lobby rows of candles blazed before images of Mother Mary and the saints. A brown-robed friar and a white-robed novitiate rustled by and I followed them to the refectory, where I asked to speak with one of the brothers. He appeared in sandals and a habit. The hood that draped his back was called a *capuce* in Italian and was the emblem of the Capuchin order to which he belonged. "Yonkers became a parish of the Capuchin order in the late 1800s when it was still farmland," he told me. There were seventeen Christian brothers at the monastery, fourteen Agnesian sisters, five Sisters of Charity, forty lay teachers, and twelve hundred children at the high school." I asked if any of the students entered seminary after the high school and he lowered his eyes behind his gold-rimmed glasses and said, no, most of them went on to community colleges. "Out of thirty-five if we'd get seven we'd be lucky. The celibate life doesn't appeal to everyone," he said.

When Ed Urich grew up in Mount Vernon in the beginning of the century there were only a few blacks, and they lived in the area around South Eighth Avenue. The Italian district was down around South Seventh. West Lincoln Avenue and High Street were German. The rich part was Chester Hill, where Bailey of the circus had an estate. At the Bronx border the old St. Paul's Church still stands, with revolutionary cannonballs stuck in the wall and Hessians buried in the graveyard.

But after the first war Mount Vernon started to fill up. Dress and electronics factories hired blacks who had fled from the rural South to an equally futureless bondage on the assembly line. The old Italian neighborhoods became black ghettos, with the Italians retaining the property and political control. Today, with almost eighty thousand people jammed into four square miles, Mount Vernon is the fifth most densely populated city in the United States. Until recently it was tensely polarized, with the blacks on the south side and the whites on the north. In the summer of 1968, after Martin Luther King's assassination, blacks broke loose at Third and Third, destroying everything in sight, just as they

170

did in other urban ghettos across the country. Today the situation has cooled and Mount Vernon is more integrated. Blacks now live on the north side, but the south side is still a turbulent ghetto with its epicenter at Third Avenue and Third Street. The current friction is between the American blacks and the new Jamaican interlopers.

In the vacant lots a couple of young men are always gathered, dribbling a basketball on the broken glass. Others are out souping up hotrods, soaping up GTOs, or simonizing Cadillacs; unable to put together a down payment on a house, the ghetto black makes his car the focus of his self-respect.

South Mount Vernon has a hangout problem. Everywhere you look somebody's hanging out. Pimps and pushers, hookers and hoods lurking in the shadows of doorways, waiting on corners like barracudas. Mount Vernon is the welfare dumping ground of Westchester County: One-seventh of the citizens are on relief, and that's probably about the number who are hanging out at any given time. The streets are never empty. Scarsdale after dark is deserted. Bedford Village rolls up *its* streets at six o'clock. But something's always happening on the south side of Mount Vernon. There may not be much glamour but there's excitement.

I had a short talk with Esther Collins, forty-one, "at your service, dahling," leaning against the door of Johnson's Country Store on the sunny side of Sanford Boulevard. She'd come up from Pennsylvania fifteen years before and was working on a bottle of Irish Rose rotgut wine that had set her back fifty cents. "It's pretty lousy here and pretty nice," she said cryptically. "You gotta make of it what you think of it. If you're lousy, your community's lousy. I think everybody gets along with me 'cause I gets along with them. If you be your own self, be your own thing, you be somebody."

Johnson's Country Store stocked fresh chitlins, liver pudding, cornmeal, sage sausages, and souse meat, only it was padlocked. So was the billiards academy across the street. Half the stores on the south side were shut on Monday afternoon. Many had windows filled in with opaque collages of color and were now selling sweet Jesus. Interspersed among a liquor store, a thrift shop, a soul-food take-out, J. C. Peace and Son Records, and J. & J. Refrigerators were the following store-front churches in a single block: Faith Tabernacle U.H.C. Inc. Church, Gethsemane Baptist

Inc.; True Born Miracle Restoration Temple; and the Holy Temple Jesus Christ Pentecostal Church. The only whites who come to this neighborhood, Esther told me, are addicts, undercover agents, and Italian slumlords after the rent.

The police aren't popular. They have set up a community-relations bureau on Fourth Street to improve their rapport with the people and to handle problems like drugs, child abuse, and prostitution. But nobody takes his problems to the police unless he's at the very end of his rope. Mount Vernon ranks first in crime in the county, "the hellhole of Westchester," as one of the cops in the community-relations bureau put it.

Few people would believe that a white man prowling around and taking notes was just trying to get the feel of the neighborhood. Finally I met someone who agreed to deliver "the inside scoop" as long as I didn't use his real name.

"So what do you want me to call you?" I asked him.

"Just call me Joe Doe."

Doe had spent all of his twenty-two years on the south side, and he seemed to know everybody and everything. His eyes were constantly on the street, reading it for any unusual movement. He had the sixth sense you develop from hanging out, like a fisherman whose eyes are always on the water. In short, Doe was streetwise. "Okay. Heah come Estherline," he said, motioning with his eyeballs to a stunning teenage girl who had just rounded the corner, her hip-hugging levis rolled up to reveal exceptionally high-heeled platform shoes. "At night she got a different name. She called Irma.

"Coupla weeks back a guy was stabbed at the Widow's Nook," Doe threw out casually. "It was all over six dollars and some cocaine." I asked him if there were any gangs on the south side and he said "Not exactly, but they's famblies. Like the Terrys. I think they're one of the biggest famblies in Mount Vernon. They come up from the South years ago, you know, and now half of the south side is related to them by marriage. The Zanfordinos—they're black-Italian—and that's another big fambly. But the Terry fambly thinks they're the baddest thing out. They like to jump people and kick ass. They have a habit of knifing people. Period. Jumpin' them in the bushes. Somebody mess aroun' with somebody's woman and he a Terry, let me put it this way: This guy is *gone*.

"But most of the trouble now comes from the Jamaicans. You have some Jamaicans feel they're more highly intelligent than blacks. They got a bad attitude. They think they're above the law. 'You can't tell me anything.' They're anti-everything. When a fight breaks out between blacks and Jamaicans in the big cafeteria at Mount Vernon High they don't let nobody in there to stop it."

Up the street was a newly opened Jamaican record store. The latest Wailer record was in the window, with Bob Marley on the cover toking insolently on a gigantic spliff of ganja, with the coils of his "natty dreadlocks" shooting out from his head like Medusan snakes. From an outdoor speaker the hypnotically insistent sprung rhythms of reggae wafted down into the Fourth Street shopping district, which consisted almost entirely of discount stores and factory outlets. Inside the small store about a dozen self-styled urban guerrillas, wearing shades and pea jackets, were going through the records.

Doe shook his head. "Jamaicans are living everywhere on the south side."*

*The above vignette, appearing in a magazine before its publication in book form, elicited a torrent of letters from angered citizens of Mount Vernon. One black woman from the south side wanted me to know that she owned her own house; she had gotten the money for it "by washing clothes and ironing for dirty people of your race while they was out having a good time." The city's mayor, Thomas E. Sharpe, was incensed that someone from a community that does nothing for the poor minorities (he was confusing Mount Kisco with Bedford) should "judge our problems." Several whites from the north side wanted me to know that their neighborhoods were as nice as Bronxville and Scarsdale, and that many of Mount Vernon's people of all races and backgrounds were working together for a better community; the Grimes Center for Creative Education, with a so-so white-black enrollment, was a particularly exciting advance. A local reporter explained that Mount Vernon was becoming paranoid about its image, because it was experiencing a massive exodus of the white middle class and loss of its tax dollars. The remaining whites lived in fear that the city would soon be overrun by blacks and Hispanics, and my article had done nothing to help the situation. An even larger number of Mount Vernonites, however, wrote or called to say that I had "told it like it is."

13 Prototypes

When Rome was at the height of its power wealthy patricians had gracious villas and shady groves to which they could escape from the pressures and the pollution of city life. These early suburbs set the tone for the ones that followed in Europe, and by the end of the nineteenth century the pattern was ready to establish itself in Westchester. By 1890 New York was well on the way to realizing its metropolitan destiny. A number of people had grown very rich, and impressive villas began to crop up in the still-green outskirts of the city.

In those days lower Westchester was still sparsely populated, and from White Plains north it was still mostly farms and was more expensive upcounty than down because it had more value as farmland. In Bronxville, just north of the city, there were a few old families with big houses. One of them was the Prescotts. They had a good-sized estate with a stone house that still stands, and they had been there since revolutionary times. About 1890, however, a man named William Van Deuser Lawrence, who had been in the pharmaceutical business in Montreal, came out to Bronxville, and, thinking he'd more or less retire, bought the old Prescott place. Gradually he got the idea of subdividing it into an exclusive community for the most prominent artists and illustrators of the period.

"I don't remember but it was forty-seven, fifty acres," Dudley Lawrence, William's grandson, told me. We were sitting in what had been once the gatehouse of the old Prescott estate and was now the office of Lawrence Properties. The interior of the building was old-fashioned and rather Dickensian with steep stairs and small, low rooms, in one of which, behind a swinging picket gate, several secretaries sat at their desks. Mr. Lawrence was a well-spoken, conservatively dressed man who appeared to be in his sixties. "Lawrence Park began in the late 1890s," he continued. "The houses were built of stucco and stone, with a lot of round towers and peaked roofs. We built an inn—the Gramatan—and town houses before anyone had heard of them. They're built up and down and have their own individual entrance. Little by little we established a business district. The apartments came—the old English country type of apartment house that is exclusive to Bronxville. By 1920 it was a well-established suburban village." Mr. Lawrence took me downstairs and slid back a glass casement which housed some of the early, now yellowed prospectuses for the new development which had been "the beautiful upland forest of an old estate." I spent an hour leafing through them in a dark wood-paneled conference room, under an imposing portrait of the founder. They made interesting reading:

Few New Yorkers know that within three (3) miles of the City Limits is a varied and undulating country, with exquisite views of hills and sea and river, winding roads under noble trees, where for miles you will not come upon a house . . .

. . . There are no fences; everyone appears to own everything. You will find the lawn of one resident winding curiously into that of another, whose grounds, in turn, merge into still another occupant's. There are no flat lawns or level gardens, but the slopes are dotted with trees, ribbed with fine rock, and starred with wildflowers.

A little lake, small, but very choice, lies in a sheltered glen whose frosty moonlight makes it an ideal place for skating revels, while there are long hillsides simply "gorgeous" for coasting . . .

Every village must now have its "movies." Here is the "Picture House." Inside is a large auditorium where only the best pictures are shown.

One brochure took the form of "a letter to Amy" from a woman who had just taken up residence in the Park, answering her friend's queries: "Society? Why, my dear, we are within twenty-eight minutes of all the society there is in the city of New York. Besides, we find that society is not altogether averse to spending Sundays in a Park, and taking tea on a piazza when the dogwood is in bloom . . . Mosquitoes? Yes, some; but not very many, and not at all big. As to malaria, of course you can have malaria here, if you want to, just as you can anywhere else; but you do not *have* to have it, and will not, if you do not deliberately court it."

With such idyllic surroundings to offer, Lawrence soon realized his dream. By 1905 seventeen artists were at work in Lawrence Park, and Lawrence proudly published a booklet showing "the retreat at which Will H. Low wields his brush far from the turmoil of the outside world" and other Jacobean cottages with leaded windows inhabited by an assortment of landscape painters, fashionable muralists, and authors of romantic fiction. The best-known artist was William T. Smedley, who illustrated Henry James's books and later painted portraits that fetched as much as three thousand dollars apiece. He lived in "The Owl House" which Lawrence built for his son. It is one of the most dramatic dwellings on the hilltop. In 1946 it was bought by Brendan Gill, a staff writer for the *New Yorker* magazine, who lived in it with his large family for the next thirty years. Gill himself has written elegantly of the place where he lived:

Lawrence Park is a model of Victorian town-planning and Victorian house-design. Its narrow, yellow-brick streets were laid out to follow the contours of the hilltop on which it was set; the houses were scattered as if at random over the rocky, wooded sites. In fact these sites were chosen not at random but with exceptional care, in order to take advantage of views, or level places for lawns, or a maximum amount of sunlight in winter. The "Owl House" in which we live was built by Mr. Lawrence in 1896. With extraordinary cunning, the architect saw to it that eighteen of its twenty-odd rooms face south;

they are filled with sunlight all winter and, thanks to a judicious employment of overhangs in the design, are screened from sunlight all summer. And the houses in the Park are joyous, are playful; it makes one feel good simply to look at them . . . With their verandas and bay windows and dormered towers and carved bargeboards and many-patterned shingles and occasional exterior sculpture, they reach out and gather one in and prompt one to share their manifold felicities.

"The feeling of the Lawrence Park hilltop," Gill explained one afternoon, "—a suburban retreat—was something new. The idea of a designed park in the 1880s was almost unprecedented. Llewellyn Park, New Jersey, in the 1860s, was the first, and Tuxedo Park had also been started. But Lawrence was taking a big speculation risk. Bronxville then was a trifling town, planted in what was still largely open country. The community which developed was linked to the station. It was an invention of the railroad. It's made up of the middle-class prosperous, rather than the rich-rich, who move out of Bronxville. It's not as rich as Scarsdale, where it's permissible for the rich to remain. 99.9 percent of the populace is Republican, reactionary, recidivist. Many of the attitudes and bigotries are those of the Civil War, although there are signs within the last thirty years of some improvement."

Scarsdale developed along similar lines, but a little later. Like Bronxville it has an attractive, homogeneous Tudor business district surrounded by beautiful private residences. Gill's description of the grand residential boulevard of Rochester, New York, could serve equally well for Scarsdale: "The big houses sat ranged in self-congratulatory propinquity on their level green lawns, like so many stout matrons seated elbow to elbow, implacably chaperoning a ball." With each mini-estate an island unto itself, Scarsdale has probably more captains of industry per capita than anywhere else in the world.

Meaning a "dale of scars," or rocks, Scarsdale was granted in 1701 to Caleb Heathcote as one of the nine manors in New York State, of which six were in Westchester. During the revolution it "knew well the tread of armies." In the 1890s Heathcote Park, a community of spacious and well-landscaped properties not unlike

Lawrence Park, was laid out by James C. Cannon. By 1922, says a historical booklet, "threatened by an invasion of manufacturing, the village passed a zoning ordinance which was intended to keep Scarsdale a village largely of one-family houses." It was during that decade that the building of large homes on small plots began in earnest. "More than anything else, perhaps, Scarsdale has plumed itself on the architectural quality of its homes. Few if any towns have sustained a higher standard."

Also typical of the 1920s was Berkeley Park—sixty-one acres of rolling farmland commanding "extensive views over the valley of the winding Bronx River" and kept intact by their owner, Colonel Alexander Crane, who had "the vision and foresight to develop Berkeley as a private community of spacious homesites." The streets wound torturously to discourage through traffic. "This careful planning is an important safety factor for children at play," the prospectus boasted. All service connections—water, sewer, gas, electricity—were underground, eliminating the need for unsightly poles and wires that would have marred the rural atmosphere. Footpaths crossed and recrossed, in a series of picturesque footbridges, a brook that had been dammed in two places to create ponds, and on whose banks weeping willows had been planted. Only thirty-four minutes from Grand Central station, Berkeley Park offered "distinctive architecture landscaped harmoniously to the surrounding countryside" and "assured privacy by rigid, permanent restrictions." A brick colonial in Berkeley sold for $27,500 in 1929, while a distinguished French-type model with limestone walls and a Ludovici tile roof went for $43,000. These houses today would probably fetch over $200,000.

The houses that managed to get built in Scarsdale during the depression were smaller. In Fort Hill Estates the "no-nonsense house" was already evolving. "The modern home combines charm and beauty of design with comfort and convenience at LOW COST," the prospectus proclaimed. "Our 1936 house outmodes in convenience the house or apartment built six years ago as completely as the latest model car surpasses the 1929 automobile." Among its amenities were "compact cheerful kitchens with their time and labor saving devices . . . attached heat . . . garages with overhead doors . . . open fireplaces . . . large liveable rooms scientifically designed to obtain cross-ventilation as well as a maximum of light and air . . . a mechanical heating system which

179

automatically keeps the entire house at an even temperature adjusted to individual taste . . . concealed radiation . . . two or three modern tile bathrooms . . . large cedar closets . . . innumerable electric outlets and many new construction features which make for efficient and economical maintenance." All this was available for $13,500 and furthermore was "situated in the heart of that part of Westchester selected by New York's wealthiest and most discriminating families as the most desirable section of the metropolitan area."

Scarsdale isn't the kind of place where you can just barge in. Nearly every house is equipped with an automatic alarm system. My introduction to the village came at a cocktail party. Most of the guests were Jewish.

Scarsdale is supposed to be running sixty-forty Jewish-gentile these days. The New York *Social Register* has no clout in Scarsdale; it is the *Who's Who* sort of prestige that is operative here. What you were doing was the main subject of conversation at the opening.

"How do you do. And what do *you* do?" I learned to say as we were shaking hands.

"I sculpt." This from a sensuous woman of about forty.

"I counsel high-school dropouts in White Plains. That and home and that's it," a pretty young wife told me somewhat apologetically.

Women in Scarsdale feel a great pressure to be involved in something. "They're all getting PhDs or have a job in psychiatric or paralegal work. Every woman's ambition is to overpower her husband," one resident told me.

This isn't going to be easy, judging by the men I encountered, all of whom seemed to be alarmingly competent. One was a poet who had composed a fugue a hundred and six sonnets long and also worked for a company, he informed me, "which makes enough carbon paper to go back and forth to the moon each year ten times. We also make inks up to one million colors. We can match to the eye's discrimination. We have fifty factories that make ink."

The house where the party took place had fourteen large rooms with leaded windows and frieze moldings. It was stucco over brick with a tile roof— "eclectic Mediterranean," as our host described it. It had been built in 1913 and in its heyday had an orchard, a greenhouse, and a staff of domestics whose quarters had been on the third floor and for whom buzzers had been installed in every room.

I was given a quick rundown on the neighbors: "On the right we have a man who has been successful in the mail-order business. He's also the president of the Friends of the Library. His wife is a sportswoman and is active in the PTA and coaches sports at several local schools. Next we have the senior executive of a New York corporation. We don't see him often but he has obviously done well because he's put in a swimming pool and added two wings. Moving up to the next couple on that side of the street— he's a senior partner of a Wall Street firm. He only comes to Scarsdale on weekends and only for part of the year. He has four other homes—one in town, one across the river, one in Miami, and one in Europe, I think. His living-room wall is *lined* with Boehm birds. He's got a lot of alarms which are going off all the time. We're the only people on the street who don't have an alarm system. His wife shows dogs.

"The couple on the corner are never here. It's a $250,000 house. She lives in New York.

"Back to the bottom left. A doctor, then a senior executive-buyer for a major retailing store. His wife is a biochemist who's done original research in hereditary diseases. The next man is president of a management-consulting firm. They're an older couple. His wife is president of the Garden Club. The next couple we know very well: The man is a senior partner of a New York law firm. His wife is the administrator of a day-care center in White Plains. The couple up from them lives next to us. The man is president of a New York textile company. The woman works in a travel agency and is an outstanding golfer."

"That's quite a line-up," I said.

"They may not be the most relaxing people to be with," he went on, "but they're stimulating and they're all high achievers— perhaps to make up for it. These are people who have made it and continue to make it. Hardly anyone I know in Scarsdale makes less than $50,000. Nobody cuts their own grass or shovels their snow. It's not done. Your 'landscape architect' comes over and does it for you. As far as I've been able to tell, and we've been here nine years, there are *no* blue-collar people in Scarsdale. Everybody's in business or a professional. They've come out from New York and, perhaps more than in any other suburb, New York is still the major force in their lives, economically, of course, but culturally, too. Everybody's a heavy patron of the arts, et cetera. Scarsdale's is an activist marketplace society. Up in your part of the county the people don't work at it as hard. Here they want to be on the cutting edge of the society. If there's a sexual revolution they want to be in on it. At a dinner party you'd better be able to hold your own intellectually, to talk about the latest books and the best plays. Money and culture are the touchstones. The money here is newer and more Jewish than in the WASP communities where it's been in the family for years and is more decadent.

"It is not ostentatious, but it is not always in good taste. You don't wear a fur coat to a dinner party, but the latest in the fashion mode. One appears in one's Bogner ski pants to play paddle tennis at the Fox Meadow Tennis Club, where the game was invented. On weekends everybody plays tennis, and it's very competitive. The last thing it's for is laughs and fun."

I could hear the names of Ivy League colleges echoing merrily from room to room, and I pitied the children who weren't going to get into them. The number of kids who don't "pan out" here is pretty high. For them Scarsdale must be an absolute nightmare. Toward the end of the evening, I met a psychiatrist. Scarsdale has a lot of psychiatrists and a lot of people seeing them. He told me about a malady of upper-middle-class children, quite common in Scarsdale, called anorexia nervosa. "99.9 percent of anorexics are teenage girls. They just stop eating, as if their constitution were saying, leave me alone, I just can't hack it. It seems to be a reaction in part to the bodily changes of adolescence, and in part to a pressured adult atmosphere. They waste away to practically nothing, but they're so beautiful, so alive and glowing, so *interested* in everything around them, that you almost don't want to cure them. It's definitely a family-related disease found more often among ethnic groups like Jews and Italians where there is a tendency to overfeed."

Windmill Farm in Armonk was built in the fifties, so the landscape has had time to recover. The Norway spruces, weeping willows, and other ornamental trees are reaching respectable size and they do a good job, along with the woods, of screening the three hundred and fifty-four nouveau-colonial homes that have been put up, to date. You wouldn't suspect that the twelve hundred and seventy acres had been "fully developed," and in a grid to boot. But only two lots, overgrown with artemisia and ragwort, remain open. Ledges outcrop over much of the property, discouraging overalteration. "We're just lucky that the land is full of rocks," a friend in the Farm told me.

The place was named for the many picturesque windmills that functioned as artesian-well pumps back when Dr. Charles Paterno ran it as a farm. Paterno was a wealthy contractor. The property is notable for its rock-work, built during the Depression by unemployed locals whom Paterno hired on a daily basis for fifty cents an hour. The high, mile-long wall, encrusted along the top with broken glass, which runs along Route 22, and the fieldstone dams and spillways that impound four small lakes, are their work. "Dad felt that by doing so the people managed to retain their pride and therefore did not have to go begging," his son Carlo wrote in a pamphlet called "Random Notes on Windmill Farm." When Paterno Sr. died, Carlo built six miles of roads and sixty houses and sold the farm to a developer. The boathouse on one of the lakes is now the Windmill Club, and the stables that housed the horses of Mrs. Paterno, who was an equestrian, have been converted into human residences.

"We have no black people. I don't know why," my friend told me as we cruised up and down the courts, ways, terraces, and lanes of the residential park. "We have Chinese. Maybe there just aren't any around here in this income bracket." It happened to be Halloween, and some of the mothers had already begun taking ranch wagon loads of minute witches and goblins from door to door. "I have never heard anyone say we don't want any blacks," she went on. "In the beginning it was pretty Waspy. Now there are quite a few Jews. And there's a pretty large IBM population. I'd say most everybody is in the forty-to-a-hundred bracket. We do have real young couples. I don't know how they do it unless they're inheriting it. I only know of one retired couple who have stayed.

"It started as the type of community you read about in *The Affluent Society*. The husbands would meet in the club car and come over for dinner and, you know, things would develop. By the time we moved here nine years ago that era was over. We always seem to miss out on everything," she said, laughing. "Now I've met a lot of people with deep religious feeling. Quite a few of

183

the people here now seem to be fundamentalists. There's an Indian cave on that woman's property. She lets groups like the Boy Scouts come and look at it. I don't see my neighbors sometimes for four months at a time. Of course, now that our son's married we don't have any connection with the schools anymore. The people are warm and friendly but they live their own lives. I have no close friends here. There are a lot of kids. It's the ideal spot for children, especially in the dead-end courts where they can play together safely. The Club is mainly for kids."

Three teenagers sped past us on motorbikes. "Recently the roads in the development reverted to the town, and the kids aren't supposed to ride motorbikes on them or on Mrs. Paterno's old bridal trails, but they do. The Windmill Association meets to discuss such things as the motorbike problem. The biggest houses are on the lakes, which are owned by the people who live on them. We can't swim in them, although skating is allowed. We might walk down to north lake in the evening in our glunky shorts and find liveried chauffeurs waiting outside for the people who are at the parties. But I've never met anybody here who has been snobbish. They've all been friendly, regular, good people."

The grid-type subdivision is pretty much a thing of the past now in Westchester, a luxury of the fifties and sixties. Rather than meting out the land in two, three, or even four-acre parcels, the current trend is now toward clustered condominiums, which are popping up in practically every township. Places like Apple Hill in Chappaqua, Jefferson Village in Yorktown, and Wild Oaks Village in Lewisboro offer the advantages of disrupting less of the land and of giving a greater sense of community than the detached single-family development.

Heritage Hills is a new condominium complex geared to the elderly. To qualify for residence one adult per couple has to be over forty, with no children under eighteen. It offers eighteen models ranging in price from the high forties to the mid-nineties and built in three configurations—Cluster, Court, and Hillview Houses, which "are designed to take maximum advantage of the site's steep terrain and consequent superb views." The houses have been perched discreetly on a broad, rolling hillside which rises from the Harlem valley and their siding of clapboard or vertical barnboard is stained with earth colors—brown, green, gray, cedar—to blend in with the woods around. The overall visual effect supports the claim that the development aims to be "respectful of the natural assets of life."

At the time of my visit, two condominiums with a hundred and fifteen units each had been completed and filled with people, and a third section was going to be open within the month. The town of Somers had voted to allow the Heritage Hills Association to assemble thirty-one hundred units on their thousand-acre property. A rec building with tennis and paddle-tennis courts and a pool was already operating, a men's and women's clubhouse was going to be built at a later date, a nine-hole golf course was now playing, with another eighteen-holer to be started soon. Each resident, after buying his unit, continued to pay a monthly Association charge which entitled him to free exterior maintenance, upkeep of his heating and plumbing systems, and a fractional shared interest in the total land. Being a member of the Association involved you in three kinds of ownership: The ground and recreational facilities were "common property"; your patio, attic, and carport were "limited common property," which meant that everyone owned a fractional shared interest in them, but you were the only one who could use them; and finally "total ownership" of the interior of your unit. It belonged to you.

Henry and Margaret Burden had just moved into a Croton, the most expensive of the Hillview models. They had been among the first ones in the courtyard, a small, intimate square cobbled with red bricks, landscaped with "the same rocks, trees, and shrubs that flourish throughout the countryside," and surrounded by other units besides the Croton—Salems, Yorks, and Ridgefields. The others were still vacant except for the Salem, where "they seem to be a nice couple," according to Mrs. Burden, who had met them only once. The Burdens were just as glad to have the courtyard almost to themselves for the time being, to be able to unpack and get settled in privacy.

I had met them just as they were moving out of their house in Bedford. They had come to Westchester in 1934 and they had always lived in a subdivision of one sort or another. "We moved from Long Island," Mr. Burden said in a gravelly, aristocratic tone. "We couldn't afford the clubs. I was in Wall Street. I started out there and ended there."

"We moved to Lawrence Farms," Mrs. Burden said. "Lawrence

185

Farms was a better-type development by the same Lawrences who had done Lawrence Park in Bronxville. It has a country club and a playhouse where Burl Ives and Henry Fonda got their start. The people who moved into it at the beginning were upper middle class, and slightly on the younger side. Most commuted.

"We were one of the few young married couples in the thirties who had the guts to borrow money and buy a house in Lawrence Farms," Mr. Burden continued. "People were buying up the little old places—the farmhouses, stable houses, and gardener's cottages, and were absolutely shocked at our choice of a house. We were of the background whose parents never did anything unusual and when we said we were buying into a development they thought we were out of our minds to buy anything as *common* as a house in Lawrence Farms. People looked down their noses at us. They couldn't understand why we would do anything so startling."

"In the early fifties," Mr. Burden said, "when the children were at boarding school, the house became too big so we moved to Bedford to a brand-new house. The land had been subdivided and several houses put up. People looked askance at *them*. We lived there for twenty-three years until I got hung up with this bum leg. There's no sense in paying those taxes for two people, and we got sick of paying a man five or six dollars an hour to come and rake our leaves."

"These are the reasons we like it here," his wife said. "It's a one-floor house, so Henry doesn't have to climb up any stairs. There are no grounds to keep up, no roofs to repair or cellars to pump out. We're only fifteen minutes from our friends in Bedford. We haven't changed our community at all. But naturally when you get to the next place you take an interest in it. We've always liked to snoop around and find out what makes things tick. We've been taking the local house-and-garden tours."

"They have a perfectly lovely rec hall," Mr. Burden went on, "and they had a party there the other night and Margaret and I went and we met some *very* nice people."

"We met people from Chappaqua, Scarsdale, and Mount Kisco," said Mrs. Burden. "We knew about eight who were here before we came ourselves. We're not *all* retired, you know. A lot of people came to have a nice place to go to work from. It reminds one of—what's that charming walled-in Medieval city in France—

186

Carcassonne, with its funny little turrets; and this carport looks like a stable, don't you think?"

"One nice thing they have is a mini-bus that runs night and day, meets the trains, and takes the ladies to play bridge at the rec hall and to Gristede's shopping center to get their hair done. Boy, the driver of that bus must hear a few things. If you want to go away for two days or two weeks you just notify the security guard . . ."

By now I was ready to take the tour. It began with the garage, whose features were described in a brochure I had picked up at the Welcome Station at the bottom of the hill. "Convenience is a major feature; residents can drive up to their houses, open the garage door electronically, drive in, and close the door without leaving their car." The large living room had double-pane picture windows and a sliding glass door leading out to a wooden deck. The room was flooded with light, yet because of its position on the hilltop it was totally private. "We don't even need curtains," Mrs. Burden told me. "Nobody can see in, but you can see out all the way up the valley to the Berkshires. We can watch the sun coming up over the hills twenty miles away from our bedroom window.

"We have an all-electric house," she went on, leading me into the kitchen. "Completely GE. It's the first all-electric house we've ever lived in. The stove, disposal, air conditioner, dishwasher—everything's underground. There's cable TV built in. You either have a cable TV or you don't have a TV. The disposal sounds like an ogre, a trumpeting elephant when it goes off.

"Isn't this marvelous?" She was showing me the fake marble sink in the bathroom. "I feel like the queen of something-or-other with this dressing room. The vents go on with the lights. That's the only thing that irritates me."

Back in the living room Mr. Burden was watching a titmouse and a nuthatch sparring at a window feeder. "There are about fifteen bluebirds flying around," he told me. "Last week we had a pair of cardinals but they haven't had the nerve to come to the feeder." I asked him what kind of a winter he thought we'd be in for. "If it gets *too* terrible we just won't go down the hill. We can call up Gristede's and they'll send it up." He paused to watch a chickadee land then added, "So we think this is going to work out."

14 Two Roads

South Bedford Road

The road I live on, only a few hundred yards from the hospital in which I was born, is called South Bedford Road or Route 172. It starts in Mount Kisco at the light in front of the Northern Westchester Hospital and ends about four miles later at the light in front of Walter Ragonese's Shell station in Bedford Village. As you start up South Bedford Road the first thing on your right is the Finast supermarket. I spend a lot of my life in there pushing my cart up and down the aisles and picking up gossip. There are other supermarkets in Mount Kisco but the Finast is the one nearest me and I feel a loyalty to it. I wouldn't think of shopping anywhere else unless the Finast were closed. I'm on good terms with the girls at the registers and with the woman behind the grill who cashes my check. We kid around a lot.

The parking lot is usually filled, and cars constantly pull in and out. The average shopper takes forty-five minutes to an hour, depending on the size of his family and on how familiar he is with the store. Sometimes people approach you as you walk from your car to the doors of the supermarket to give you a free sample of some new product or ask for a donation for underprivileged children. I am still using my complimentary canister of an antiperspirant. As you step on the rubber mat an electric eye releases the door. You walk up to a string of shopping carts, shake one loose, and proceed past the pink-veined caladiums—a bit of the Amazon—in the house-plant and garden-supply section, to the fresh fruit and vegetables. Two short, wide women in babushkas have congregated here, chattering to each other in Italian, examining each cucumber carefully before making their final decision. In front of the celery case a little come-on sign says, "Stalk no further—meet the best bunch around."

Sale items are usually displayed at the end of the aisles. Market research has proven that anything put on an end display will sell better, even if it is kept at the same price. People buy on impulse. If there's an advertising campaign on television there is usually movement on an item. During December Canada Dry advertises "Have enough on hand for Christmas and New Year's," so the quart bottles of ginger ale are placed on an end display, and marked down from thirty-nine cents apiece to three for a dollar. "Or like last Halloween," an assistant manager of the store explained, "when they had the Kraft caramels on TV and they had the recipe for caramel-covered apples on the bag, you put the caramels on an end display. That's just simple psychology."

The packaging is vital. One wants a bright color that will stand out. "In recent months," the assistant manager went on, "a new brand of catfood called Meow-Mix has really taken off. It seems to sell better than the old, established brands. The only possible explanation for this is that it comes in a shocking yellow package. After all, it's all the same to the cat, isn't it?" One tries to mix the colors up a little, too. In the coffee aisle, for instance, one doesn't put the cans of red Martinson and red Savarin together; one puts the blue Maxwell House cans in between. In the peeled-tomato aisle the color mix reaches perhaps the highest degree of taste and harmony in the store.

The music at the Finast is rented from a service. It is chosen for its mood. It must be cheerful. "You don't want to depress people. Keep 'em happy. Light Broadway shows, things like that. It's kind of dingy without it. It keeps the help in a good mood, too. There are more than fifty employees in all. A lot of them are part-time. High-school students who start work after school lets out and are home in time for supper. It's an excellent place for them to learn a little fiscal responsibility and how to deal courteously with the public. You get to meet a lot of people. There is, of course, a lot of pressure on you. High above the aisles there's a little booth, and somebody's always up there, watching you. He's up there not only to keep an eye out for shoplifters but also to make sure the employees aren't goofing off. Some supermarkets have a system of mirrors that enables him to see down every aisle, so he has a full view of the whole store from up there, but the Finast isn't that uptight."

In Westchester small jars and cans don't move as fast as medium and big ones because it's a family-type population. Milk moves faster by the gallon than by the quart. In the cities people buy the six- and seven-ounce cans of peeled tomatoes; here there is more turnover with the sixteen-ounce cans of *pomodori pelati* (of which, in recognition of Mount Kisco's large Italian segment, the Finast stocks eight different brands). And because this is an affluent area, the store sells more of the national brands than its own—more Maxwell House than Finast coffee, even though the Finast is cheaper. It also moves a lot of beer and club soda.

At the end of aisle four a small soul-food section caters to Mount Kisco's black population.

It is Friday afternoon and there is congestion at the registers. Basket after basket overflows like a cornucopia to get the family through the weekend. Each checker is backed up by a bagger to make things move faster. I am the only male in the line. I take in the headlines of the *National Enquirer,* next to the *Reader's Digest:* FANTASTIC NEW SALARIES OF THIS YEAR'S TOP TV STARS. KIM NOVAK IN LOVE WITH HER VET. "Could you step on it a little bit, please?" the lady behind me says to our checker who is obviously new to the job, just feeling her way around the keys. The goods of the lady ahead of me move forward a little on the black conveyor belt. I place a rubber bar to separate hers from mine and begin to lay mine in the opening. The girl rings up my purchases. It comes to $17.76. We giggle over that. The bagger bags. The checker hands the tape receipt along with an envelope and explains the rules of the Gigantic Grocery Giveaway.

All I have to do is write my name, address, and phone number on the back of the envelope, put the tape inside, lick the flap, and drop the whole thing in a big box over at the bank that has just opened next door, and I could win back the $17.76 I just spent.

There will be two winners a week for the rest of the month. The checkers who rang them up will each receive a twenty-five-dollar bond. At the end of the month one name will be drawn from the big box and that person will win a three-minute shopping spree at the Finast, compliments of the bank. The spree is known as a supermarket "sweep."

I didn't win. The lucky lady was Mrs. Letitia Napolitano, who owns a beauty parlor in Chappaqua. They let her come in a few days beforehand and plot her route. When the day of the sweep came they cleared the store. She stood with her cart poised at the beginning of aisle one and when they told her to go, away she went. She got butter and cheese in the dairy and then she raced over to the meat department and practically cleaned it out, grabbing hams, steaks, and roasts right and left. Then she raced over to the frozen turkeys and swept up a few of them. Then she threw in a little shrimp, crabmeat, and other expensive stuff. Then her time was up. They rang up the contents of the exhausted woman's cart and it came to $403.33. You wouldn't have believed a cart could hold that much.

Soon after the Finast, South Bedford Road leaves the world of commerce to spend the rest of its existence winding through beautiful, rolling country. Two miles down, the road goes under Interstate 684, a six-lane superhighway pushed up from Harrison a few years ago. 684 cost more than 1.5 million dollars a mile and while the need for it was indisputable, it went through some of the best land around and got a lot of people upset. The most expensive stretch was probably just south of South Bedford Road where the Interstate was blasted through Chestnut Ridge. Chestnut Ridge is a great crystalline mass of Fordham gneiss, which is just about indestructible. Somehow, though, a great chunk of the hill was removed and bulldozed into the hollow just north of it. I remember that hollow very well. South Bedford Road used to go down into it and the descent was so steep that in icy conditions cars would often go out of control when they got to the bottom, and there were a lot of accidents. Down in the hollow there was an imposing white-columned house and a pond with a little island that had a Japanese pagoda on it.

Interstate 684's impact on the region was dramatic. South Bedford Road became its fourth exit and in no time at all changed from a quiet country road into a heavily traveled truck route. Fifty years ago it was an event for the people on the road when five cars went by in one morning. Not long ago, I took out my pocketwatch and listened to the whooshes that went by in one minute and I counted twenty at 10:26 on a Wednesday morning. South Bedford probably carries about fifteen thousand vehicles a day. One could learn much about what is happening to Westchester just from studying this road.

Every minute or so a tractor trailer runs by the house. The windows shake; the whole house shakes. It was built, like many of the old houses, not more than five feet from the road. The road was dirt then. The internal combustion engine was seventy years from being envisioned. During the Revolution, a detachment of redcoats led by Colonel Banastre Tarleton, the dashing "Green Dragon" who left dozens of women brokenhearted in his wake, may have marched up this road on his way to burn Bedford (this is a matter of considerable local debate: the colonel may have marched up another road, several hundred yards away, and, even more dismaying, it may not have been his detachment that did the burning at all, but another one that came nine days later).

Recently a large black mudguard with the word THEURER stamped on it detached itself from one of the trucks and landed in the pachysandra, a few feet from the front door. I have also in my possession a red flag from the Wheatland Pipe Co. and a collection of hubcaps.

One icy February morning an eighteen-wheel diesel, headed for the Grand Union warehouse on the other side of Mount Kisco, jackknifed in the straightaway just below the house, careened into the embankment, sideswiped a passing car, flattened the guard rail, snapped a telephone pole in two, and finally came to rest on its side, wheels spinning. The driver, who was thrown fifty feet through the windshield, was miraculously "more shook up than anything." Dozens of sides of beef that had been hanging from hooks inside the box were ejected onto the pavement. Within minutes, the police had set up flares and were directing traffic. Then two firetrucks and an ambulance came screaming up the road. The traveling salesman in the car that had been sideswiped was extricated in time to see his rented car and all his samples burst into flame. Three firemen attacked the blaze with their extinguishers. Then Walter Ragonese came with one of his elaborately decorated Holmes tow-trucks, extended the hydraulic boom, retracted it, and drove the wreck away.

Someone came from McDonald's and everybody stood around drinking coffee and discussing between mouthfuls of Big Mac what they were going to do about the overturned truck. It wasn't till nightfall that they succeeded in righting it and getting it out of the road—first the box, then the cab.

Starting at about six on weekday mornings the trucks are joined by legions of commuters hurrying to their trains into the city, and I can see their tight faces behind the windshields, already set upon the day before them. A bit later the schoolbuses canvass the street corners of Mount Kisco and come lumbering up the road headed up to Fox Lane High School. The men who perform essential services—the plumbers, carpenters, electricians, treemen, land-scape-maintenance men—pass in pick-up trucks whose doors are inscribed with their names, services, and telephone numbers. And by midmorning the housewives have done their hair, donned their pants suits and dark glasses, and are ready to face the world. All day long the road belongs to their great big ranch wagons, to the mailman's jeep, and the brown van of the United Parcel Service. And up and down the road high-school students and dropouts lope along the shoulders, wheeling around to stick out their thumbs at you.

The plant life along the shoulders is interesting. Almost every member of the community is an immigrant: the velvet-leaved mullein which sends up late in the summer a stalk higher than any other nonwoody plant in Westchester except for the wild lettuces; the escaped day lilies and pachysandra, the English ivy smothering the well-made Italian walls, running wild into the woods and climbing up the trees; the solid half-acre thickets of bittersweet and all the sun-loving composites like the dandelion and the black-eyed Susan. All these ruderal plants followed the migrations of man. It is this kind of marginal habitat—neither woods nor open field—where the sparrow hawk hunts, hovering in place some twenty feet above the ground. Red-tailed hawks, too, keep close watch on the movements below them from their post in a tall tree.

There are two swamps along South Bedford. Skunks, raccoons, opossums, and deer are often hit as they are crossing the road at night to drink in one of the swamps and are blinded by headlights. A lot of dogs get killed on South Bedford Road, too. The other morning I heard someone hit the brakes and I looked out and there was a young German shepherd lying on the road. The pup lived another minute. His tail was wagging in his own blood. Then it stopped. I called the police and they took the carcass away in a green plastic bag. I've lost two cats on the road. Cats aren't very smart about cars. They'll walk out on a quiet moonlit night and—bam! Crows know about cars and so do mourning doves. I've never seen a dead crow or a dead mourning dove on the road, although both birds spend a lot of time flying up from traffic. Chipmunks are worse than cats. Squirrels aren't much better. They'll misjudge a leap from one branch to another, fall into the road, scramble to their feet, see a car coming at them, scamper frantically one way then the other, and finally stand directly in the face of death, paralyzed by indecision. According to a recent survey conducted by the U.S. Department of Transportation, about one million "pieces" of wildlife are killed on the road each year. Cars are now the number-one predator of many carnivores and ungulates. The traffic on South Bedford contributes its share. The animals learn respect for moving metal objects or they die.

North Bedford Road

Highway strips are beautiful places for observing the sky. They're so wide open, built usually on flat stretches with the low businesses set back behind arid fields of tarmac or desiccated earth. Breathtaking sunsets unfold before you. Cloud formations ascend like fabulous snowpeaks. Turkey buzzards teeter overhead on wide, feathery, uptilted wings just as they do over the marketplaces of Latin America. But who looks up? The splendors of our civilization are too mesmerizing. There's Waldbaum's, the first store to open in the new Shopper's Bazaar, all covered with red, white, and blue crepe. They made it look like a barn. They tried to capture the essence of early America. There's the big white cone on the Carvel ice-cream stand. There are the golden arches in front of McDonald's.

Our local semilawless street of chance is called North Bedford Road. It's about two miles long and runs from Mount Kisco to Bedford Hills, parallel to the railroad tracks. It's actually part of Route 117, which runs all the way from Katonah to Tarrytown, but you could just say "the Bedford strip" and people around here would know what you were talking about.

It's mostly devoted to fast-food places, chain stores, and automotive businesses: body shops, pit stops, car washes, used-car lots, parts places, muffler places, tire places, front-end alignment places. The fast-food place that does the fastest business, is, of course, McDonald's. They post the scores of eight high-school football teams in McDonald's. There's always a line of people waiting to satisfy their craving for beef. Mothers stuffing their kids with Big Mac to keep them quiet. The craving is so strong that it transcends class barriers. Everybody from hilltoppers to young blacks with braided hair eats at McDonald's. A whole colony of English sparrows hangs out at McDonald's waiting for crumbs. A few years ago two men with pillowcases over their heads entered McDonald's at 11:45 p.m., fifteen minutes before closing. There were no customers, only the two counter girls and a young assistant manager. One of the hoods pointed a handgun while the other produced a third pillowcase into which he emptied the contents of the registers. Then the hooded duo slipped back into the night as suddenly as they had come. They were on foot. Unfortunately for them, the pillowcase the loot was in developed a leak, which enabled the police to follow a trail of bills and coins back to their apartment on Elton Street.

Then one day McDonald's burned to the ground. The building was "totally involved," according to the local paper. It was an electric fire that started in the wires of one of the machines that made French fries. People went through beef withdrawal for several months until the new building was ready.

My favorite fast-food establishment on North Bedford Road is Vic's. Vic's is a 1957 International van that's parked in a vacant lot across the street from Caldor's. It's painted red, white, and blue, and flies an American flag from each fender. The inside is done over with red-and-white-checked contact paper and green wall-to-wall carpeting. It's got an electric heater that enables it to stay open all year round. Vic sells steak-and-pepper and sausage-and-pepper wedges. "Other states call them subs, heroes, hoagies, and grinders," Vic explained. He also sells barrelhead root beer, hot dogs, and chile dogs. He makes in his opinion the World's Greatest Chile. "My food is guaranteed not to break, rust, collect dust, rip, rattle, or tear you apart," he exclaimed. "And further-

196

more, my chile's made with meat, not beans." He makes up ten gallons of chile every two weeks at home. Victor Fanucci was formerly a cook in the army. Now he's Slic Vic on the Bedford Strip. His kitchen-on-wheels rocks with the traffic and is open ten to five. "Never fear, Vic is here." He is known from Katonah to Mount Kisco and from Mount Kisco to New York. They come from Mahopac and Peekskill just to eat his steak wedges. Greater metropolitan truck drivers pass the word through him; he delivers their messages. "Look, I been on the strip eight years. When I came here there was no McDonald's, no Burger King, no Chuck's Steak House. *I* was the only place that offered hit-and-run food. I'm a cook and not a thinker but I can tell you the traffic has doubled."

Change, flux, turnover—this is the dominant theme of the strip. Back before the war you could have rolled a bowling ball down North Bedford Road and not hit anything. The whole road was lined with trees. The first development was residential. Joseph Chamberlin was a carpenter and builder who had been born in 1888, the year of the blizzard. In the twenties he put up a number of brown shingle houses and rented them. Most of his tenants were schoolteachers. They were clean, educated people who took good care of their houses. Chamberlin built his last house in the early thirties, then turned to cars because there was no housing market.

Years ago, coming down from Bedford Hills, the first thing you came to was not the car wash and the tractor place; it was a ball field. They called it the AC Field. You either played ball there or at the high school. Then right next to McDonald's where the pool place is now there was Toni's Rest—a candy store with two gas pumps out front. Between the AC Field and Tom's Rest was an open space. Now you have the car wash, McCormack's Jeep and Mercury, Bedford Hills Beverages, Martebano's clothing store, Martebano's gas station, Wayside Lighting, and the pool place. Years ago the next place on the right was L. H. Brooks Dairy. They bottled and pasteurized and did everything right there. Now it's Art's Linoleum and there's a body shop and a garage in another part of it. Then the next place on the right, where you have Zeus Subaru, used to be Jake Several's. That was a fruit stand and they squashed apples right on the premises and you used to get cider there. All the rest was open. Now you've got Fein's Dog and Cat Hospital, Toyota North, Barker's, Adams Pontiac. Right on the corner where Adams is now you had a little blacksmith shop. It was operated single-handed by an Irishman named Phillip Hourican. He was a real craftsman and he did the horshoeing for all the hilltoppers. And that only takes us halfway down one side of the strip.

When Joseph Chamberlin got out of construction he started with a used-car lot across from the AC Field. His son Ken joined him when he got back from the war and in 1957 Chamberlin *père et fils* took on a Studebaker dealership and operated it until Studebaker went out of business in 1966. Then they went back to used cars, many of which were Studebakers. My father was among those captivated by the Studebaker mystique. Over the years Ken Chamberlin has sold him four of them, three of which he used as "station" cars. Ken's been out of the business for a few years now, but he still thinks the Studebaker was the best car ever made.

"Studebaker and Packard were two of the oldest companies," Ken told me. "The Studebaker Corporation in South Bend was a father-son-grandfather kind of deal. There was pride in the workmanship of each car. The Studebaker had a full frame like a ladder. It was heavier-gauge metal, a very sturdy-built car. The eight-cylinder was the most economical one you could ever drive. I've never seen a Chevvie or a Plymouth or a Ford be as good on gas. It had overdrive which most cars didn't have. And it had something else that no other car ever came out with called a hillholder. It was another little cylinder in the brake system connected to the clutch so you could hold a car on the hill without having to have your foot on the brake pedal. It left your right foot free to be on the gas pedal. It was for women who burned out their clutches or stalled trying to get started off a hill.

"Studebaker's engineers were years ahead of everybody in styling. You remember the Bulletnose? It looked like a P-38 Lockheed twin engine plane without the propellers. That was in 1950. Years later other cars copied it. In 1947 Studebaker came out with the blunt front end and the blunt back and a lot of glass. Other cars didn't copy that till 1949. The 1953 Studebaker had a sloping hood and back and other cars like Dodge and Plymouth didn't copy that till 1956. It seemed like Studebaker sort of set the style for a number of years. And of course in 1959 they came out with the little Lark and two years later Plymouth came out with the little Valiant, Mercury came out with the little Comet, and Ford came out with the little Falcon.

"A Studebaker car was quality. The chrome, the metal, the upholstery. Like the hard rubber armrest. You couldn't wear through it.

"Of course," he conceded, "the others cars have had a few good years, like the Chevvies along in 'fifty-five, 'fifty-six, 'fifty-seven. That was a good-rolling car and had real good lines. In the sixties the others were coming in and foreign cars were breaking into the market and Studebaker just couldn't keep competing from their dilapidated plant in South Bend. So they moved to Canada and the American public didn't want to accept the fact that the cars were being made in Canada. But the truth is that they were only being *assembled* in Canada." Grief choked Ken's voice for a moment before he was able to continue. "A lot of your dyed-in-the-wool Studebaker owners wouldn't buy a Studebaker any more. Their loyalty was to the United States. But the farce of the whole thing was that South Bend was still the headquarters, where the parts were being made, so it wasn't really a Canadian-built car *per se*."

Ken sold Chamberlin Motors a few years ago, retiring while still in his fifties.

"I still wholesale part-time a couple of days a week—just off the cuff, just to keep busy. Occasionally I reshape the car myself and retail it. I don't sell a car unless I've gone through it myself. 'We stand back of the quality of this car.' That was Studebaker's slogan. They put it on a sticker in the windshield of every car. That is my policy, too."

One Saturday afternoon, like a good suburbanite, I went to Caldor's, the biggest and busiest establishment on North Bedford Road. My radio was tuned to the local station, which runs a "pet parade": "Lost in Katonah, a long-haired cat named Zowie." I pulled in between a beaten-up tow-truck that said "Blood Brothers Auto Wreckers OW 3 5200" and a ranch wagon that had a bumper sticker on which the female candidate for a local town board promised "I'll do my level best."

Perhaps 60 percent of the thousand or so cars in Caldor's lot were ranch wagons. Wagons are the most ubiquitous rigs in Westchester. Many of them had simulated wood side-paneling. I decided to go around and make a list of the different makes:

Grand Torino	Monaco	Century Luxus
Country Squire	Pinto	Sport Wagon
Commuter	Kammback	Custom Suburban
Sport Suburban	Rambler "Classic"	Matador
Safari	Town and Country	Rotary Wagon
Grand Safari	Sport Satellite	Concours
Gran Torino Estate	Caprice Estate	
Suburban Estate	Townsman	
Kingswood	Belair	
Revel Cross		
Country	Caprice Estate	
	Wagon	
Biscayne	Ambassador	
Satellite	Vista Cruiser	

As I looked up from my task a boy in a white apron was pushing a string of maybe fifty abandoned shopping carts back to the supermarket. An individual who did not inspire trust came up and offered to beat out the dents in my fender for five dollars. "No thanks," I told him. "I just came to buy some socks."

15 The Brutal Commute

Contrary to popular notion, New York is not where everyone in Westchester does business. In fact less than a third of the county's work force is employed in the city. According to a recent bulletin from the county Planning Commission, there are about 370,000 jobs in Westchester. Only 120,000 residents commute out; 70,000 nonresidents commute in, and 7,000 new jobs are added each year. In 1930 only ten percent of the county's work force commuted, although in bedroom communities like Chappaqua and Pleasantville the percentage was as high as sixty-six and two-thirds. The image of the bleary-eyed commuter waiting at the platform persists as part of suburban mythology, although as more big corporations locate in the outskirts there is less need for the journey.

My father has been commuting with dignity for thirty years. For many of them he boarded at North White Plains. The drive along Route 22, along the shimmering Kensico Reservoir and under the great dam, was a pleasant way to start the day. It took twenty minutes. Like many commuters, my father drove to the station in an old secondhand car, leaving the more presentable rig with his wife.

201

Over the years he has gone through eight station cars: two Ford sedans, a Hillman Minx, a Ford station wagon, a red Studebaker sedan, a green Studebaker Lark station wagon, a Corvair that was destroyed by a flood in 1968 while parked in North White Plains, and a little brown Studebaker sedan. He went to North White Plains because there was a greater choice of trains and because the overall journey was shorter. If you boarded anywhere north of there, you had to wait at North White Plains for several minutes while they switched engines from a diesel to an electric for the final stretch into the city. But in the early 1960s the New York Central Railroad started running FL-9 diesel electric locomotives on the Harlem Division. They are equipped with a third-rail contact shoe so you don't need overhead wires. Now it's quicker for my father to get on at Bedford Hills, and he has more time to work.

While the commuting fare has multiplied by a factor of five since my father has been paying it, the commuting time has not improved since 1847. In fact in the days of steam when the tracks were new and the trains sleek and efficient, it was an hour's run from 42nd Street to Mount Kisco. Now only the fastest express trains make it in an hour and three minutes. There used to be a gang every five miles who walked their section daily making sure the ballast was right beneath the ties so the trains didn't bounce up and down the way they do today and carrying long-handled wrenches to tighten any loose bolts. Now it's done with mechanical "tie-tampers" and "rail liners." There isn't the human involvement, an employee told me, or the personal satisfaction that everyone who worked for the railroad once felt. The trains aren't running as smoothly as they used to because for many years the tracks weren't kept up.

Steam engines were much more exciting, especially the 3300 series "hand-fired bombers" which rushed through the night, sparks flying, passing one hamlet after the other and consuming a hundred and thirty-five scoops of coal an hour. Arthur Bernhard, a retired railroad man who lived in Bedford Hills until he moved to California a few years ago, has never gotten over the time he was twelve and got to ride in one of the last of the hand-fired bombers sitting next to the engineer because Bill Healy was a friend of his dad's; during the construction of Grand Central Station his daddy switched tracks for trains laden with bedrock that Healy drove in. It was just Arthur and Bill Healy, deadheading from Yonkers to Harmon. "That wail of the whistle, two long, one short and one long," Bernhard wrote in reminiscence of the trip which he had printed for his friends, "is a sound that one never forgets.

"How does the engineer know when to blow the whistle? Some distance before the crossing is a sign adjacent to the track with a large W painted on it. When he passes it he pulls the whistle cord and sends that wonderful sound across the countryside."

The 3300 series hand-fired bombers were replaced by the 5200 series of 1926 which had automatic stokers, delivering coal to the firebox by means of a screw-type feeder located under the floor. By 1947 the use of steam engines on the Harlem Division had been discontinued altogether. Today's whistles are electric imitations of the old steam ones.

I was only a regular commuter for several months one summer but I have often joined their ranks. I'm on a first-name basis with Lou, the giant of a man who sells newspapers and coffee at the Mount Kisco station and enlivens the waiting room with fox-trot music from his radio. The station is a popular campaign stop for local politicians. In season they can be found at the door promising to reintroduce trust into politics and government and handing out leaflets with pictures of themselves. It is an all-male scene except for a few prim women. Conversation is minimal except for a few life-of-the-party types one wants to strangle. Some are not yet awake. Some wear funny crumpled hats in an effort to make it somehow more human. Others stand like infantry at dawn waiting to be shipped to the front. For some the commute is only part of a larger, savage work pattern, like the man I know who is the vice-president of a big company yet continues to catch the six o'clock train each morning, arriving with striped two-blocked tie, wings of collar pinned tight, and gold watch fob draped across front of vest, fully two hours ahead of everyone who works for him. For some the commuting becomes addictive. Some even look forward to it. "Regular commuting is relaxing," my father told me. "It's the late hours that get you."

What the passengers do on the train has not changed significantly since a survey was made of their activities in 1942. "49% read, 82% of these read papers, 25% do nothing, 8% smoke regularly, 11% talk, 3% don't even remember what they do or

203

don't do." To these activities I would add playing poker, drinking in the bar car, sleeping, looking through the dirty windows, and working. The invention of the pocket calculator enables the commuter to play with big figures on the train and has been a boon for those who want to keep working. On some trains, which offer business courses, you can even improve your education. But the big thing is reading the paper. It is understood that one doesn't talk in the morning, and the cars are silent except for the sound of the pages of the *New York Times* and the *Wall Street Journal* being turned. Commuters are important to the paper business because many go through two newspapers a day, using a lot more than the five hundred pounds of paper which the average American consumes in a year.

The marshy expanse between Mount Kisco and Chappaqua is seldom noticed by commuters except in July and August when it glows with thousands of lavender spikes of purple loosestrife. Once at dusk I looked out and saw the intent white form of an egret, an uncommon bird in Westchester, hunting among the loosestrife stalks for frogs. After taking the train for years one gets to know what's coming around each bend, the garden plots just into Chappaqua, the elderberry clusters at Hawthorne, the blank headstones in front of the monument dealer at the Kensico Cemetery, the billboards in the Bronx, the ailanthus and the weeds along the tracks. In winter the journeys are made in darkness and the commuter seldom sees his home by daylight until the weekend.

One evening as I was coming back from New York the train stopped unexpectedly. It stood in White Plains for ten minutes until the commuters began to rattle their papers impatiently. A black silence fell over the train as the passengers realized that the siren they were hearing was that of an ambulance. The conductor opened the door and said, "Does anybody know————?" and a voice behind me said, "God, what a lonely place for it to happen."

Complaints about the rail services seem to monopolize conversation whenever two or more commuters are gathered together, and breakdowns happen regularly enough to stoke their ire. One Friday evening nothing seemed to go right, and the train was an hour and forty-nine minutes late. Penn Central published an apology in the local paper:

TO REGULAR PASSENGERS OF TRAIN NO. 967 (the 5:39 p.m. to Brewster):

We apologize for the approximate two-and-a-half hours of delay many of you suffered last Friday evening before making your destinations between Hawthorne and Brewster. No "post-game" analysis can make that suffering easier, but you should know the separate incidents which contributed to your tribulation.

Your 11-coach, two-engine train lost 7 minutes in Grand Central Terminal because the brake would not release on the rear coach; another several minutes in traffic congestion because switch trouble near Scarsdale required using only one track.

Both engines failed south of the White Plains station shortly before 7 p.m. because of a burnt power cable and other electrical malfunctions.

Efforts to transfer you to the 6:00 and 6:29 p.m. trains to Brewster were frustrated by both those trains being already loaded to capacity; the 7:13 p.m. to Brewster took some of you.

At 7:05 p.m. a relief engine was dispatched from North White Plains yards to accommodate you; it suffered its own engine failure before leaving.

Finally, our dispatchers cancelled the southbound 7:02 p.m. from Brewster at North White Plains (where its passengers could connect with other trains), and used its engines to turn and pull your disabled train. The heavy load cost you another 19 minutes. It all added up to 149 minutes late at Brewster.

Admittedly, a very bad night of service to you. We are very sorry.

METROPOLITAN REGION

But the days of the gray-flannel cattle cars may be numbered. Within the next few decades, the *Economist* predicts, the number of commuters may be down to a trickle.

"Telecommunications should gradually allow an increasing number of breadwinners to live in whatever communities they wish to form and to 'telecommute' daily into their New York offices from homes in Tahiti or the Alps." The businessmen will be able to conduct deals with other parties whose faces are projected on screens he has flicked on in his living room. If telecommutation does displace commuting, it will have a drastic effect on Westchester life, on the housewife and the children who are used to the father being away most of the time, doing something down there of which they have only a vague idea. But I don't think anyone will be throwing away his timetable in the near future.

16 Coming Attractions

One afternoon I was shown to the office of the County Executive, Mr. Alfred Delbello. The walls were lined with congratulatory communiques from schoolchildren and various framed prizes including the "Outstanding Young Man of the Year" award which Mr. Delbello had won a few years before. Like Mr. Vergari, his district attorney, the County Executive had risen by sheer drive and capability from humble Italian-American beginnings in Yonkers to the county's highest office. At the time of our meeting he was just thirty-six, with glasses and a strong, handsome face—a down-to-earth, relaxed pragmatist who struck me immediately as someone who had the situation under control. I asked him what he thought was going to happen to Westchester County and he asked me how long a period of time was I talking about. Thirty years, I said.

"In the next thirty years you are not going to see that much change," he began. "It will not be a city of Westchester. In the last two years there has actually been a loss of population," he said.

"In order to remain static," he went on, "we need to build about three thousand new housing units a year, because every year we lose fifteen hundred units due to fire or dilapidation. Another three thousand units are needed to house the same number of people because every year the number of people in each unit goes down. In the last twenty years the size of the average household has dropped from 3.7 to 2.4. Therefore we are losing people. They are very identifiable: the young marrieds who can't afford it here so they move to outlying counties like Putnam, Dutchess, Orange, or Rockland. Everything indicates that the county is going to become older and poorer. You will see a growth of the poor and the elderly population and the minorities will grow because they're usually the poor ones. This spiraling effect will tend to drive urban centers into a substandard state which tends to feed on itself, to attract more poor and more minorities. In the first half of the next thirty years you will see urban centers become more rundown. After fifteen years of this cycle I think some of the initiatives that we're working on will start paying off. Our redevelopment program, calling for new housing and housing rehabilitation—I think that will start taking hold.

"Seventy percent of the population lives south of Route 287 on thirty percent of the land," Mr. Delbello continued, "and that balance is going to remain. Most of the ailing municipalities—Yonkers, Mount Vernon, New Rochelle, Port Chester, North Tarrytown—are south of 287. Some of the river towns like Peekskill and Ossining also exhibit symptoms of urban decay. But that's pretty good for four hundred and fifty square miles of land. And what's nice is that they're all separated except for the two cities to the very south. Mount Vernon and Yonkers compound each other's problems. I believe they need major redevelopment. The old centers have to be torn down and rebuilt according to a design that will lead to a better way of life. Peekskill is well on its way to recovery. It's receiving more money per capita than any community in the country. Port Chester has no drive. Yonkers is a political problem. Mount Vernon I don't see an answer to. I don't see any aggressiveness on the part of the municipality to deal with its problems.

"I don't think the character of the north-county will ever change. It will always be open and residential. You might see a few more industrial parks, corporate headquarters, and condominiums, but there will be no great outgrowth in the north-county. No more great subdivisions. The economy is creating a shock in the development people thought was going to happen.

The zoning, the high cost of construction, and social attitudes are making it hard on the developer. We're reinforcing this no-growth trend with our master plan, declaring areas that are 'forever rural.' We will not be investing our capital dollars in the development of these areas."

I couldn't agree completely with Mr. Delbello's position that nothing is going to change in northern Westchester. It seems that every time I look out, there's another house furtively wedged in some corner of the landscape, or another new shopping mall. It seems inevitable that the faceless suburbia of Hartsdale, Elmsford, and New Rochelle will eventually creep up into these parts. And while it is true that the northern communities haven't yet experienced that much physical change, psychological forces are already at work, transforming villages and hamlets into movie sets and caricatures of themselves. This has already happened to Bedford Village, Pound Ridge, and, to some extent, Chappaqua. Mount Kisco, Katonah, and Bedford Hills continue to hold out.

As a general rule, to get an idea of what any given Westchester town will be like in ten years, one need only drive ten miles south. White Plains is a glaring example. Like Mount Vernon ten years ago, it is seeing an increase in poor minorities, a flight of the white middle class, a deterioration of public transport, and withdrawal of mortgage money and investment capital.

After my meeting with the County Executive I talked with Peter Eschweiler, Commissioner of the County Planning Board, who gave me a pile of the trend analyses that his office prepares. A picture of the main factors, endogenous and exogenous, which are going to either stimulate or inhibit the growth of Westchester, emerged.

NOTES ON THE PROSPECTS OF WESTCHESTER COUNTY

1. ENDOGENOUS FACTORS WHICH ARE PROBABLY
   GOING TO INHIBIT GROWTH AND DEVELOPMENT
   A. THE LACK OF HOUSING
      In order for the population of Westchester to remain static, three to four thousand housing units, as Mr. Delbello pointed out, must be built per year. At the moment, less than fifteen hundred units—or 0.5 percent of the existing housing stock—are being built annually,

although the provision of shelter, in terms of the cash flow generated by mortgages and rentals, continues to be the biggest business in the county. Since 1960 rents and the cost of a house have gone up at twice the rate of the cost of living—another prohibitive factor.

Growth results from either natural increase or in-migration. In the last decade the birth rate (the number of births per one thousand people) in Westchester has fallen off because people have been living longer, and the fertility rate (the number of births per thousand women between the ages of fifteen and forty-nine) has fallen off because of birth control. People, even in Westchester, aren't having as many children. At the same time there are a great number of single households in the census, three times as many as there were in the sixties. People aren't jumping into marriage as they once did. In fact, more and more people, as everyone knows, are getting divorced. Every time a marriage breaks up it creates a need for new housing. As a result of all these factors, the household size is down to about two and a half and getting smaller by .066 persons a year, and it's taking more units to house the same number of people.

In the late 1950s the population of Westchester was growing by ten percent a year. By the sixties, when six thousand new units were being built annually, it was growing by one percent a year. In the early seventies it went down to one-tenth of one percent, and by the middle of the decade it hit zero and started going into decline. These demographics are reflected in the thickness of the Westchester telephone directory, which doubled its size in the last two decades and has now stabilized at about three and a half inches.

Future in-migration, as it is called, will be a function of whether or not it can be accommodated. At the moment, housing construction is at an almost complete standstill.

According to the County Planning Board, Westchester's population will stay the same until at least 1985, but there will be changes in its composition, with losses in the under-twenty group and gains in the twenty-five to forty-four and the sixty-five and over groups (the last of which is living in paid-up houses). Whites will decrease and non-whites will have increased by 14.6 percent by 1985. The median age will rise from thirty-three in 1970 to thirty-six in 1985. This belies the notion many people have that the great American migration to suburbia is continuing with unabated vigor, at least in Westchester. The single-family subdivision, which uses up the greatest amount of land in the shortest amount of time, has been a thing of the past in Westchester since about 1968. The luxury condominium market enjoyed a flurry of activity in the early seventies; but it too seems to be suffering from the recent recession. Not long ago Apple Hill, an adult condominium village in Chappaqua, went bankrupt. Moreover, few municipalities can offer the large-scale services that clusters of condominiums require.

B. PHYSICAL LIMITATIONS ON GROWTH

Because of its crystalline substrate, Westchester has no porous rock layers or aquifers in which water can collect. Ground water depends on the fracture systems in the bedrock; one man may have a lot while his neighbor could drill indefinitely without results. (The year-round temperature of the ground water, by the way, is fifty-three degrees. Anything higher than that is an index of pollution.) While the north-county is studded with lakes and reservoirs, the abundance of surface water is an illusion. Back in the nineteenth century agents from New York cleverly bought up all the watersheds, while the area was still rural and people in Westchester didn't realize their importance. As a result most of the county's water is imported from the Catskills and the Delaware Water Gap. Yonkers, Mount Vernon, White Plains, and Scarsdale are served by a forty-eight-inch pipeline from the Kensico Reservoir above White Plains, which is fed mainly by the Catskill Aqueduct. The north-county communities are served mostly by private wells, supplemented by the Croton Reservoir system, whose quality is not good. Most of them have no water lines and can't afford them. By the end of a dry summer the situation in places like Bedford had become critical. The town has had to tap into the wells

211

of the women's prison in Bedford Hills to keep going. So water—or the lack of it—is a major constraining factor against development.

Hand in hand with the hydrologic problem is the one of sewage disposal. Many streams in the north-county are being polluted by leechings from thirty- and forty-year-old septic systems which are no longer doing the job. After heavy rain, when the contents of hundreds of septic systems are flushed out and carried downstream, the smell in the Harlem valley, parts of which are flooded with up to four feet of water, can be noxious. Storm-water runoff has become a serious problem not only in the urban sectors but in the suburban ones, because the manicured lawn is almost as impermeable as pavement and generates almost as much runoff.

Until more is known about the carrying capacity of the land in terms of its ability to provide water and to dispose of effluent, the county has wisely declared a moratorium on large-scale development while it waits for the answers to come from a "208" study funded by a million-dollar grant from the Environmental Protection Agency. Meanwhile the *state* has decided to require all developments of fifty units or more to have their own tertiary treatment plant, a prohibitive item for most developers. So water and sewage act as a natural barrier to further growth in the north-county, whose communities can't afford, with their current tax-base, urban amenities such as a thirty- or forty-million-dollar filtration plant, which might open the region up.

With most of the level land spoken for, the lack of suitable building sites is another inhibiting physical factor for nonresidential development, which requires extensive floor space and ideally a slope of no more than four degrees. Private homes can be, and are being, built anywhere.

C. THE SOCIAL STRUCTURE

Civilization in Westchester has articulated itself in a series of concentric rings radiating outward from the city, with the poor nonwhites in the inner ring and the rich elite on the outer edge. The social strata and ethnic divisions in the suburban and exurban rings are quite rigid, but the one attitude that seems to be shared by all is that no one wants more people coming in. Most of the people one talks to express strongly worded no-growth sentiments. Town meetings are often used to harass prospective developers, and even the local businessman sometimes has to fight to get approval for a small improvement like an extension of his parking lot. Some merchants complain that unreasonable use of land-use controls under an environmental banner in Westchester these days is stifling free enterprise. As a recent bumper sticker I saw said: IF YOU'RE OUT OF WORK AND STARVING EAT AN ENVIRONMENTALIST.

In hard-core suburban Mount Pleasant the citizens have formed a group called the United Homeowners. While it has the reputation of being opposed to everything that comes along, in speaking with their president, Tony Saitta, I could appreciate their position. About ten thousand families live in the township. The organization draws its following—several thousand citizens—from the unincorporated outlying areas of Thornwood, Hawthorne, Valhalla, Bear Ridge, and Hardscrabble, where the most restrictive zoning is one acre. Most live on lots of less than one acre, having extricated themselves with considerable difficulty from Yonkers, Mount Vernon, the Bronx, or the congested areas of Long Island. They love their hard-won parcels and their relatively verdant surroundings, and they want them to stay that way. "We see nothing wrong with remaining a residential area," Saitta, who describes Mount Pleasant as "the Switzerland of Westchester County," told me. "We serve our regional obligation with hospitals, penitentiaries, cemeteries, nursing homes, schools for handicapped children, with every institution you can name. What we want is to put in the hands of the people the major decisions of how the town is going to grow." The United Homeowners are not opposed to everything, Saitta explained, only to multifamily housing, "not because we're scared of people," but because they want to preserve the semirural character of the landscape.

213

They have nothing against single-family homes or the high-revenue low-service-cost "campus office" type of land use where only ten percent of the property is built on. They supported, he pointed out, the IBM Trade Center which went up recently in nearby North Tarrytown. The organization feels that the planning board is "several notches" more enthusiastic about development than most of the town, and that the notion that growth produces revenues turns out more often than not to be a myth when one adds up the roads that will have to be improved, the utilities that will have to be updated, and the additional policemen, firemen, and teachers who will have to be hired. A statement by Commissioner Eschweiler, that the single family house in the county generates more cost for education than school taxes, would support this. "One day the people who call us selfish and reactionary will thank us," Saitta predicted. "If we can keep Mount Pleasant a green space where families can raise families, time may prove us to be rather prophetic as far as the development of Westchester County is concerned."

In exurbia, territoriality is a serious matter. The exurbanites' greatest tool for keeping out undesirables and development of any kind is zoning. The segregated social structure can be maintained indefinitely as long as the zoning can be held at four acres. The defenders of "exclusionary zoning," as it is often called, point out that you could double the population without changing the zoning, and that if you relaxed all zoning restrictions but upheld the environmental criteria for development, the sewage, water, and soil conditions would all tend to dictate the construction of no more than one house for every four acres. This is obviously not true, however. The earth has yet to open and swallow the skyscrapers in Manhattan, which were built on what was originally similar terrain.

Both the "208" study, when it comes out, and the County Master Plan, which has declared "forever rural" the townships east of Interstate 684 and north of Route 287—Pound Ridge, Lewisboro, South Salem, and half of Bedford—are probably going to reinforce the status quo. Of course a future administration could have a different

Master Plan; one should always be suspicious of the word "forever."

2. INHIBITING EXOGENEOUS FACTORS
   A. POSSIBLE DECAY OF NEW YORK AREA

   The big unknown, of course, is the continued social and economic viability of New York City, New York State, and the Northeast in general. If New York collapses, it could go either way for Westchester. If the big corporations in New York relocate in the county or within commuting distance, Westchester could actually benefit. But if the corporations leave the Northeast altogether, Westchester as it is today would fall to pieces in short order. Commuters are Westchester's biggest export. It is their income that supports the county's inflated economy.

   B. THE ATTRACTIVENESS OF OTHER PLACES WHERE LAND AND LABOR ARE CHEAPER AND TAXES LOWER

   The New York income tax, in order to support the various social reforms the state is trying to bring about, has become itself a prohibitive factor. According to one article, an executive can save five thousand dollars a year by moving out of Westchester to New Jersey or Connecticut. Other articles rave about the "sunbelt," that part of the South which includes such cities as Houston and Birmingham and has been growing steadily since the invention of the air conditioner. If solar energy can really be harnessed, that region's possibilities seem limitless.

   C. WATER

   Most of Westchester's water comes from the other side of the Hudson, but there is no guarantee that this will continue to be. At present Nassau County draws from its own wells, but this practice has lowered the water table so much that some parts of the shoreline are experiencing salt-water intrusion. There is talk of running a pipeline from the Catskill-Delaware water system to help them out. If that happened, there would be even less water for Westchester.

   D. ENERGY

   Exurbia, it has often been pointed out, was built on cheap energy. If this were no longer available (one

215

remembers with a shudder the gas lines of a few years back), the north-county would go into rapid decline, and the south-county, with at least a semblance of a public transit system, would probably benefit. The great suburban boom, when woods and country clubs were being turned right and left into subdivisions, took place before anybody had ever heard of an energy crisis. Everyone began zoning for development, and the profligacy of the zoning map led to an inefficient land-use pattern with respect to transportation.

One of the great flaws in the geography of Greater Metropolitan New York, in terms of energy wastage, is the mismatch of residential areas and work sites. White-collar workers go down to the city while unskilled workers come up from the Bronx to work in the factories of lower Westchester. But the increasing scarcity and costliness of fuel could well reverse this pattern. A low-income worker isn't willing, for obvious reasons, to travel as far to get to his job as an upper-income person. A secretary in Westchester, for example, generally works within twenty minutes of her house. Whatever new jobs are created are liable to be in the existing centers of population, where they can be served by mass transportation—and this is something that the county government is encouraging as a matter of policy. The net effect would be growth and prosperity for lower Westchester, and stability or decline for the north-county.

E. VARIOUS OTHER INHIBITING FACTORS

These include the Environmental Protection Agency's already-mentioned prohibitively expensive sewage treatment requirements and the state's protection of all wetlands fifty acres or larger.

3. ENDOGENOUS STIMULATING FACTORS

A. THE AMENITIES

These include the excellent schools, the safeness and the physical beauty of the environment, the suburban location, the radial highway system which makes it not only easy to get in and out of New York City but a relatively pleasurable motoring experience. One qualification of the last point: While it is easy to travel up and down the county, the concentric links to the radials were never built,

216

except for Route 287. It is exasperating and time-consuming trying to get across the county, and it is doubtful, furthermore, that the connecting links to the radials will ever be built now because of the inflated cost for rights of way and the difficulty of changing the zoning. So there is not likely to be much interaction between such cities in the suburban ring as Ossining and Stamford, Connecticut. If the railroad comes back in vogue as the result of an energy shortage, and the trucks that now carry most of the freight are retired from the roads, the county will see a different pattern of development. Industrial sites along the tracks, which have no great value at the moment, will suddenly be in great demand.

B. POSITIVE ATTITUDE OF LEGISLATORS

The county does not, of course, want to see itself go down the drain, and capable leaders like Mr. Delbello are looking for ways to insure that their jurisdiction remains viable and attractive. The county announced recently, for example, the creation of a new agency called the Westchester County Industrial Development Agency, which will be able to provide tax-exempt bonds and federal funding for the financing of various types of commercial development and public works like roads, sewers, water supply, etc. This may have some effect in offsetting the quarter of a million jobs lost in the New York region from 1969 to 1974. But the county government is realistic, too. As one planner put it to me, "Westchester is no longer like a beautiful young girl who has had so many offers that she can afford to be capricious."

C. POSSIBILITY OF MORE LAND FOR DEVELOPMENT

If the philanthropic institutions and nature sanctuaries which hold some of the key open spaces in the county are put back on the tax rolls, many of them will have to give up their land. And of late the municipalities, feeling the crunch themselves, have begun to put pressure on some of them. In order to get your land off the tax rolls, you have to prove that you're up to some good. You have to be *doing* something with it. "Empty" land just sitting there won't do.

4. EXOGENOUS STIMULATING FACTORS

A. "BUSTING THE ZONING"

There are several groups, most notably the Suburban Action Institute, which are trying to do away with the existing land-use structure. A study of northern Westchester towns which this organization put out recently found that 16.7 percent of the total residential acreage is zoned for four acres, 34 percent for two acres, and 29 percent for one. Since an acre lot in Westchester that can be built on can fetch as much as twenty thousand dollars, one can see that the Institute has a valid point when it calls the zoning "exclusionary." Established to encourage greater opportunity for minorities and poor people by breaking up segregated land-use patterns, the egalitarian group has challenged the constitutionality of low-density zoning laws in Pennsylvania, New Jersey, and Connecticut, and recently brought legal action against the zoning in Brookhaven, Long Island. How far they will get in Westchester remains to be seen, because constitutionally the decision of what to do with the land resides with the municipalities. The most that can be done at the moment is try to shame the town into putting up some tasteful low-income housing.

B. PRESSURE THROUGH COURT DECISION ON LO-CAL HOUSING POLICIES

There's no way a poor family can be accommodated these days in most of Westchester without federal assistance. As the *Wall Street Journal* reported recently, "The booming suburban economies have created numerous semi-skilled jobs that could be filled by ghetto dwellers except that there is no place for them to live." In a recent Supreme Court decision a Chicago suburb was practically commanded to take on a public housing project. While it is still not possible for the federal government to *order* a town around, it can make things very unpleasant for the town in other ways. And practically speaking, the only way low-income housing will come in is through the courts, since the local legislators, responsive to their constituencies, are in no position to encourage the project.

C. CHANGING FEDERAL POLICY ON FUNDING OF PUBLIC UTILITIES

The long-term bonded public-works projects that West-chester needs but cannot afford—sewage treatment and filtration plants especially—may receive federal assistance.

If these amenities are installed, they will alter the current picture, eliminating the existing physical restrictions of water and sewage disposal.

It should be clear by now from this simplistic list of its prospects that there are a lot more inhibiting factors at the moment than there are stimulating ones, so nothing drastic will probably happen for a while.

Personally, I find the coming attractions rather attractive. I must take issue with the visiting reporter from the *Economist* (the British observer always seems to take the blackest view of things here) who writes of "the probably failed experiment of suburbia as a mechanism for living together." Wasted, yes, and rather passé, I'll agree. But by no means at the end of its rope. The fact that civilization probably isn't going to make any devastating incursions into the region in the immediate future is encouraging for the long-term interests of the organism in these parts. We need all the time we can get.